Preface

The first sound is always the same. Heel clicks, sharp and deliberate, echo across the white marble of the plaza. The sound does not belong to you, not anymore. It belongs to the place, to the silence that holds every step accountable. The air at Arlington feels different—heavier somehow, as if it remembers. The Tomb of the Unknown Soldier is not just stone and crypts; it is a living reminder of sacrifice, a place where silence is sacred, and where devotion is measured one step at a time.

Walking the mat as a Sentinel is pure devotion. From my first trembling step onto that silent plaza, rifle in hand and uniform pressed, I felt the weight of more than duty—it was a vow etched in each heartbeat. Every twenty-one steps, every deliberate pause and sharp turn, was a silent promise to the Unknowns: You will not be forgotten.

It is difficult to explain to those who have only seen it from behind the rails and chains. Tourists watch for minutes, maybe an hour, and leave with photographs. To us, every walk was a lifetime compressed into silence and motion. The Tomb strips away excuses, pride, and shortcuts, demanding only one thing: perfection. And when you learn to live with that standard, it never leaves you.

The silence of Arlington is unlike any other silence. It is not emptiness. It is weight. It presses into your chest until you can hardly breathe, but it steadies you all the same. You hear the shuffle of shoes on stone from the visitors who gather behind the chains. You feel the sun beating down on your shoulders in July or the bitter cold in January, cutting through every layer of the wool uniform. You taste sweat on your lips as it drips from your brow, knowing you cannot move to wipe it away. Even the rifle in your hands feels different here, heavier, though nothing about its weight has changed. Everything at the Tomb feels amplified. The uniform itches more. The shoes press tighter. The moments stretch longer. What seems simple to the outside eye is, to us, a battle of will.

I remember the first time I saw the mat, before I ever walked on it. Its black rubber surface stretched in front of the marble crypts, worn smooth by countless footsteps. It looked ordinary, but to us, it was hallowed ground. Every scrape in its surface marked devotion. When I finally stepped onto it, I felt the weight of history in the soles of my shoes. I was not just representing myself, but standing in the place of hundreds of Sentinels, and of thousands lost nameless on battlefields across the world.

When I began writing this book, I wrestled painfully with whether to do so at all. Tomb Guards are trained—no, conditioned—to deflect attention away from ourselves. Our sacred duty is to the Unknowns, not to our own stories. To write a memoir felt, at first, like a betrayal of that silence, a crack in the armor I had learned to wear. For years, I said almost nothing about what it truly meant to walk the mat. Yet the weight of my experience grew heavier with time. Eventually, I realized that telling this story is not about me; it is another way of honoring the Unknowns. Their sacrifice is the reason we walk. Their absence of name, their absence of recognition, demands that we live in a way that aches to remember them. By sharing what the Tomb taught me, I hope to ensure that their story and these lessons of devotion and resilience reach far beyond Arlington.

I write for the Unknowns, whose silent sacrifice gave meaning to every step. I write for my fellow Sentinels, past, present, and future, who know what it is to endure the crucible of the mat. I write for soldiers in every generation, who carry their own burdens of sacrifice and resilience. I write for my children, who may one day understand why their father's standard will always remain perfection.

The Tomb taught me lessons that no other duty station could. The lessons were simple in words but relentless in practice. Precision in action meant that every detail mattered. From the angle of a rifle to the distance between steps, nothing was too small to demand perfection. That same precision later kept me alive in Afghanistan, where checking a weapon twice or confirming a radio signal could mean the difference between life and death. Strength in silence meant more than standing still. It was the ability to endure, to hold fast when every fiber of your body wanted to shift or quit. That silence taught me patience, a discipline that carried me into leadership.

On patrols in Afghanistan, it meant listening to my soldiers before speaking, weighing their words before making a decision. It taught me that real strength is not noise but steadiness. Devotion beyond self was the heartbeat of the Tomb. The Unknowns gave everything, even their identities. Our job was to honor them, not ourselves. The lessons I learned did not stay behind in

Arlington. That devotion shaped how I later approached leadership, family, and therapy: it is never about you. It is always about those you serve.

The Tomb does not just shape you as a soldier; it reshapes you as a human being. I arrived in Arlington with determination but little patience. I left as a Sentinel, with discipline carved into me like stone. That standard—my standard—followed me into every chapter of life. In Afghanistan, it gave me calm in chaos. As a father, it reminded me to be steady for my children. As a therapist, it gave me the patience to listen deeply and honor the burdens my clients carried. In business, it taught me that success is not about shortcuts, but doing the right thing every time. Many of my most important lessons were whispered in silence on that marble mat.

To truly grasp what the Tomb means, it is necessary to look to its broader context. To understand the Tomb, you must also understand its history. It is not merely a monument but an active guard post, a living tradition. Orders are written, reliefs are assigned, guards are posted twenty-four hours a day, seven days a week, through every storm and season. Since March 25, 1926, a Sentinel has never failed to walk the mat. Through hurricanes, snowstorms, and even during 9/11, the watch has never stopped. To stand that watch is to step into a tradition larger than yourself, to inherit the weight of nearly a century of unbroken vigilance. The men and women who earn the badge join a lineage measured not by fame or glory but by silent devotion. Out of the millions who have served in the United States Army, fewer than a thousand have ever stood this post.

This historical weight is magnified by the Unknowns themselves, who represent the highest cost of war. The World War I Unknown lies directly beneath the Tomb. Behind it rest the Unknowns from World War II and Korea, and once, from Vietnam. Their silence speaks for all who were lost without names, for every family who never received certainty of where their son or daughter fell. To guard them is to carry that memory into the present, to ensure that their sacrifice is not blurred by time. It is to live with the constant reminder that freedom has a price, and that the price is borne not only by the fallen but by their families, and by every generation that follows.

Standing the watch means enduring punishing weather until every muscle begs for relief. In summer, the mat feels like a skillet; the wool uniform clings, and the sun presses on your shoulders, reflected back to you from the marble. In winter, the icy wind cuts through layers, snow gathers in your hat, freezes on your lashes, and stiffens your sleeves. Rain seeps through everything, chilling you to the bone. Yet you keep moving, twenty-one steps, twenty-one seconds, then back. The public may not see the blisters, shivers, or sweat. They see only precision. That is the point. The Unknowns did not choose their conditions of sacrifice, so we did not choose ours.

There were moments, deep in the endless rhythm of the mat, when self-doubt hit like cold rain. Was I worthy of this ground? Could I really endure it, day after day, month after month, for years? Every Sentinel faces those shadows. The Tomb does not flatter; it exposes your flaws, fears, and cracking points. It pushes you until either you break or you cling to a hidden strength you never knew you had. For me, that strength emerged slowly, like the sunrise, born of hours spent polishing shoes through exhaustion, of fixing a crease long after hope had faded, until I understood: the mat stripped me down, yes, but only to rebuild me with purpose.

There were mornings when the plaza belonged only to the faint blue of dawn and the breath of the trees above the amphitheater. On those days, before the visitors arrived, the world felt paused, just a thin ribbon of light over Washington and the long rectangle of the mat beneath my feet. I remember the warmth of the rifle in my hands from the quarters below, the faint scent of oil on steel, the creak of leather when I shifted my grip. Even the smallest sounds—my own breath, the click at the apex of a turn—seemed to hang in the air and float toward the crypts. I learned to count in heartbeats. The twenty-one seconds were a metronome no one else could hear.

At other times, the plaza belonged to families. I can still see a little boy in a collared shirt, standing on tiptoe behind the chain, saluting with a hand that wobbled as he tried to make it sharp. His mother stood behind him, eyes bright with tears she tried to hide. She whispered something I could not hear, and the boy's arm trembled but did not drop. We are trained not to break bearing, not to look directly, not to react. But even without turning, you feel the presence of people—grief and pride radiate, and sometimes the past seems to step forward and stand beside you.

Not every day was solemn. There were moments of almost normal life under the quarters, quiet jokes exchanged when the door closed, the rustle of garment bags, the hiss of steam as an iron passed over cloth. We lived in a world of lint rollers and shoe polish, of measuring tapes and the staccato rhythm of heel clicks practiced on concrete. New guys asked the same questions I had once asked, and the older hands had answers ready, delivered without heat, because someone had done the same for them. The routine became a kind of comfort: inspect, prepare, walk, repeat. If I did the small things right, the big things took care of themselves.

Still, doubt crept in at odd hours. Sometimes it surfaced during a silent guard change, when time seemed to slow down and every second stretched out. Sometimes it rose at two in the morning, when you were bone-tired and your hands shook, and the only light was a sliver seeping under a door while you rewove a stray thread on your uniform and told yourself you would not, could not, lower the standard. There is a kind of prayer in that stubborn promise: not a prayer for yourself, but for the Unknowns, that you will be worthy of them.

The Tomb taught me that endurance is often quiet. It is not the roar of victory but the slow, steady refusal to give up. It is learning to hold still when everything inside you wants to move. It is learning to keep your voice calm when others shout. It is being the same person, disciplined, precise, devoted, when the plaza is full and when it is empty. That steadiness became a compass I carried into every other part of my life. When fear showed up in Afghanistan, the silence of Arlington steadied my hands. When I sat with a client and listened to a story they had never told, that same silence made room for their pain to emerge. When I built a company from scratch and the numbers didn't add up, the lesson remained: do the next right thing, the exact right way, and then do it again.

Sometimes I think about all the names we do know and how they point to the ones we do not. The Tomb holds four crypts, but in a way, it holds thousands. The Unknowns become a stand-in for every soldier who vanished into the fog of war, every family who never got more than a telegram and a lingering ache. Walking the mat, you learn that your body can keep moving in the worst weather, and you learn that your heart can keep honoring people you will never meet. It is a strange combination of humility and pride: you are nothing, and you are part of something unbreakable.

People have asked me if guarding the Tomb changed my faith or rewrote my beliefs. It did something quieter than that. It gave my beliefs a posture. It taught me how to stand—how to embody values with my body, not just my words. Honor is not a speech; it is the angle of a rifle held steady for an hour. Devotion is not a slogan; it is the twenty-second pause that never wavers. Respect is not a feeling; it is the way your shoes meet the marble without a stutter.

Years after I left Arlington, heel clicks still echo in the empty halls of my memory. The lessons refuse to fade. Yet memory does fade, and if I do not put these stories into words, I fear they will vanish without a trace. Silence can be both a balm and a curse. I write because the Tomb taught me the truth of duty: it outlasts pain, and it outlasts pride. I write because my children deserve to know not just what I did, but why each stubborn standard and sleepless night mattered. They deserve to know that their father's devotion, the grinding insistence on order, the refusal to yield, was shaped in holy quiet, for men who surrendered everything. I write because soldiers, those beside me, those before, those yet to walk, carry burdens too heavy for words. Maybe mine will ease their load or at least remind them they are not alone in the weight.

I dedicate this book to the Unknowns, whose sacrifice gave meaning to every step. To my fellow Sentinels, whose heel clicks still echo in my memory, and whose devotion binds us across generations. To the soldiers I served with in Afghanistan, especially those who never came home. To my children, who will one day read these pages and know that every sacrifice was not just for country but for them, so they would grow up in freedom, knowing what honor means.

The Tomb of the Unknown Soldier is not about me. It is not about the Sentinels who guard it. It is about the Unknowns—men who gave everything, even their names. But in guarding them, I was changed. This book is my attempt to capture that transformation, not for recognition, but so the lessons of the Tomb will endure. Because in the end, perfection is not a finish line. It is a standard. And once you have walked the mat, you carry that standard for life.

Table of Contents

Preface _____ 1

Table of Contents _____ 10

Introduction _____ 11

Chapter 1 – A Legacy of Service _____ 18

Chapter 2 – The Path to the Tomb _____ 27

Chapter 3 – Trial by Fire _____ 46

Chapter 4 – The Badge Earned _____ 66

Chapter 5 – The Sacred Duty _____ 81

Chapter 6 – Stories from the Tomb _____ 89

Chapter 7 – The Bond of Sentinels _____ 103

Chapter 8 – Mental Toughness _____ 114

Chapter 9 – Honor and Sacrifice _____ 122

Chapter 10 – Carrying It Forward _____ 130

Conclusion _____ 139

Copyright Page _____ 141

Dedication _____ 142

Introduction

The first time I visited the Tomb of the Unknown Soldier, I was around five or six years old. My memories are hazy, as you'd expect from a child that young. I remember the sun being bright and the marble seeming almost blinding in its whiteness. I remember the chain barriers that separated the public from the mat, and how quiet the people around me became, even if I didn't understand why. But I did not grasp the meaning of what I was seeing. For me, it was simply another place my parents had taken me, another stop on a trip I barely understood. I left with no sense of the weight that hung over that ground.

I never returned to the Tomb again until I was a soldier. By then, I had completed basic training, stood in formation until my legs burned, and learned what discipline and drill really meant. When I saw the Tomb as a young private in the Old Guard, it was no longer just a marble monument or a distant ceremony. The silence struck me differently. The sharp uniforms, the rifles, the exactness of every step—all of it resonated with the discipline I had begun to understand in training. The plaza no longer felt like something distant or abstract; it felt alive, as though it was demanding something of me that I couldn't yet name.

Only later, after deployment and combat, did I fully understand the burden the Sentinels carried. But even in those first moments as a soldier, standing before the Tomb, I recognized that this was no ordinary posting. You cannot truly understand the weight of silence until you have been tested by it, until you stand in a place where silence means respect, precision means devotion, and one careless step could dishonor men who gave everything.

I believe fate brought me to the Tomb. In basic training, I asked a simple question about the Old Guard, not realizing how much power those words would carry. That question became my small step into a river of destiny that swept me forward. By asking, I set in motion a series of events that would place me in the 3rd U.S. Infantry Regiment, "The Old Guard," in February 2007. Looking back, I wonder: did I choose it, or did it choose me? Perhaps both. In the Army, many choices are made for you, but sometimes, paths seem to open when you lean toward them.

The Old Guard is unlike any other unit in the Army. Most soldiers think only of deployment, training rotations, field exercises, and combat readiness. The Old Guard performs those tasks, but it also assumes ceremonial responsibilities that are unlike anything else in the military. To serve in the Old Guard is to stand at the intersection of tradition and duty, where history is alive in every action.

I remember the day I received my orders. Other soldiers in my basic training class were headed to line units, airborne units, and cavalry regiments. When they heard I was bound for the Old Guard, their reactions were mixed. Some were impressed; it was known as a prestigious posting. Others looked at me with pity, assuming I'd be stuck polishing brass and parading around Washington, D.C., instead of doing "real soldiering." They didn't understand that the Old Guard deployed too, that its standards broke soldiers faster than combat units sometimes did, and that hidden within those ceremonial uniforms was a crucible unlike anything they'd experience.

When I arrived in D.C., I was assigned to the Regimental Orientation Program, ROP for short. ROP is where the Army begins to strip away the general training of basic training and replace it with the precision required for ceremonial units. I graduated as an honor graduate, which gave me confidence but also placed me in the spotlight. It was there, still riding the satisfaction of graduating, that I asked about the Tomb of the Unknown Soldier. I did not make a formal request or raise my hand to volunteer; it was simply a question: what was the Tomb, and how did it work? That curiosity alone was enough. In the Old Guard, sometimes curiosity is a quiet way of volunteering. Fate had spoken, and I stepped forward.

The Tomb is not just a posting. It is a crucible. It is a place where discipline is tested beyond what seems humanly possible. It demands silence that feels heavy on your chest, precision so exact that the smallest error disqualifies you, and devotion so consuming that nothing else can come first. At the time, I didn't understand that silence. I didn't understand what it meant to embody sacrifice in each step. But I would learn.

One night during training, as midnight stretched on, I finally began to feel the weight of responsibility. We were required to repeat the sequence of twenty-one steps, each measured to the inch, down the length of the mat, over and over again. There was no applause, no audience, no encouragement. There was only the harsh glare of a spotlight and the watchful eyes of the sergeant. His voice cut through the silence, swift and direct, leaving no room for excuses. Every mistake was caught. Every hesitation was magnified. The heel clicks echoed in that space like a metronome of devotion, and under that pressure, I began to understand. This was not about me. This was about them, the Unknowns.

That night, I realized that walking the mat was more than a ritual. It was a sacrifice embodied in motion. Every pause, every turn, was a living memorial. It was a lesson that would reach far beyond Arlington's marble into every part of my life: into combat, into leadership, into family, into healing.

This book is more than a memoir about standing guard. My main message is that the Tomb's lessons reach far beyond military service. Values like discipline, honor, and resilience are not limited to those who serve—they shape every aspect of life. These values prepared me for the demands of war, the challenges of coming home, the responsibilities of fatherhood and business, and the practice of healing as a therapist.

By sharing my journey, I hope readers see that the Tomb's teachings are universal: the mat never truly ends. These lessons—endurance, honor, devotion—apply to all of us, not just those who wore the badge. The main message is that, whatever the odds, the lessons learned at Arlington can help anyone persevere.

I remember the soldiers I served with who faced impossible circumstances and still refused to give up. I remember clients I have counseled who carried trauma heavier than any rucksack, yet who found ways to keep moving. I remember my own doubts, my own failures, my own nights staring at the ceiling wondering if I could keep going, and I remember that I had once walked twenty-one steps forward, paused twenty-one seconds, and turned, again and again, in the face of every doubt. That standard remained with me.

For soldiers facing adversity, it is crucial to remember that perseverance and discipline are not optional—they are the path forward. You don't survive the crucible of the Tomb without them, and you don't survive combat, or family struggles, or personal battles without them either. These qualities, ingrained at Arlington, became indispensable tools in every part of my life.

Precision in execution means that the small things matter. I saw soldiers lose their chance at the badge because of a thread out of place, a shoe not polished to standard, or a rifle carried at a fraction of an angle. Those details may seem trivial to outsiders, but to us they were everything. Later, in Afghanistan, I understood why: small details save lives. A missed check on a weapon, a sloppy formation, a rushed plan, those are the things that get men killed. Precision is not just ceremonial; it is a matter of survival.

Resilience in adversity means persevering when you want to give up. I watched men quit Tomb Guard training, not because they weren't capable, but because the pressure broke their will. Others endured, not because it was easier for them, but because they refused to let themselves quit. I carried that lesson into firefights, into sleepless nights with crying children, into long days of paperwork when running a business. Resilience is not glamorous. It is stubbornness baptized in sacrifice.

Silent strength means listening before acting. At the Tomb, silence is sacred. You do not fill it with words. You fill it with presence. That taught me to lead differently, to listen to my soldiers before issuing orders, to listen to my clients before offering advice, and to listen to my children, even when my instinct was to lecture. True strength is not in speaking louder than everyone else. It is in hearing what others cannot or will not say.

Selfless service means remembering that it is never about you. At Arlington, you are reminded constantly that the Unknowns gave everything, even their names. Compared to that, your sacrifice, missed holidays, sleepless nights, hours of polishing, is nothing. That lesson carried me into combat, where the mission and the men came before myself. It carried me into counseling, where the client's healing matters more than my ego. It carried me into fatherhood, where my children's needs always outweigh my comfort.

Consistent discipline means holding the standard even when no one is watching. At the Tomb, you are inspected endlessly, but the real test is not inspection; it is what you do in the dark, when no sergeant is looking, when it is only you and the marble. Do you still polish to perfection? Do you still press the crease sharply? Do you still hold the rifle exact? That kind of discipline is what sustains you in life when there are no immediate rewards, no applause, no recognition. It is the foundation of trust, of character, of leadership.

These principles are not just lessons; they are foundations. They were written into me in silence and carried forward into every chapter of my life.

And so, I invite you to step into this story. To walk with me along the mat, into the quarters, into the storms and the sun. To follow me from Arlington to Afghanistan, from the crucible of the Tomb to the chaos of combat, and later into the quiet work of healing. Along the way, I hope you find pieces of your own story reflected here. Because the Tomb is not only about those of us who wore the badge. It is about every soldier who gave all, every family who carried loss, every leader who wrestled with responsibility, and every person who faced a trial and chose not to quit.

The mat never truly ends. It simply changes shape. For me, it became the rutted mountains of the Paktika Province, the offices of graduate school, the late nights at a desk building a company, the quiet moments holding my children. For you, it may be something different. But whatever your path, the lessons endure.

This book is my attempt to carry those lessons forward. To ensure the Unknowns are never forgotten. To demonstrate how perfection, although never fully achieved, remains the standard. To remind us that silence has a strength of its own. Most of all, to prove that honor and sacrifice are not concepts buried in marble—they are living, enduring truths.

Chapter 1 – A Legacy of Service

The sound of packing tape tearing across cardboard always echoed through half-empty rooms. Friends became phone numbers that eventually faded into silence. The posters came down, the mattress leaned against the doorframe, and the house was stripped bare. As the last box labeled *PROPERTY OF U.S. ARMY* left, I felt like a ghost, already forgotten where I was leaving, not yet part of where I was going.

Every move had its rhythm. After the tape and the boxes, the next phase always started the same way. The transition was predictable: first came the orders, casually announced at the dinner table by my father, as if he were just reading the weather report: *'We're headed to Missouri,'* or *'Pack it up, we're going overseas.'* He never delivered the news like a choice. It wasn't. The Army dictated our lives, and we fell in line. My mother would sigh, already calculating schools, packing lists, and goodbyes. My siblings and I sat quietly, pretending to shrug it off, though inside I felt the ground tilt.

Then came the packing days. Strangers in uniforms wrapped everything in endless layers of paper. Even a lamp or a cereal bowl disappeared into boxes bound for storage. The walls of cardboard grew higher, transforming the house into something unfamiliar. By day's end, only the ache in my chest felt familiar.

The worst part was the waiting. After our home was stripped, we slept on borrowed cots, eating takeout on paper plates amid the hollow echo of empty rooms. It was too early to belong to the new place, too late for the old.

School was always the hardest. Walking into a new classroom with the smell of floor polish clinging to my clothes, I could feel eyes on me before I even sat down. The teacher would pause at roll call, stumble over my last name, then announce to the class that I was "new." That word followed me like a curse. *New.* Not local. Not permanent. Not one of them.

Kids have radar for differences. Mine was my accent, shaped by wherever we'd last been stationed, whether Alabama drawl, Midwestern flatness, or clipped tones from South Carolina. Sometimes, it was the clothes that stood out. More than once, I heard it: Army brat. It meant I'd be gone soon, so why bother?

There were times I fought back in little ways. Sometimes I'd adopt an accent just to see how long it took people to notice. At other times, I leaned into being the "weird Army kid," telling stories about places we'd lived as though I were a world traveler instead of a perpetual exile. But most of the time, I just kept my head down and tried to adapt.

Every once in a while, though, I'd find another kid like me; someone whose dad also wore green, whose life was measured in duty stations instead of zip codes. We recognized each other instantly, not because of what we said, but because of what we didn't need to explain. We both knew the ache of tearing tape, the hollow echo of an empty house, the quick goodbyes. With them, I didn't have to pretend that moving was no big deal. We both knew the clock was already ticking.

More often, it was just my siblings and me navigating another fresh start. Riding our bikes in a new neighborhood, I wondered how long before we'd leave again. The answer was always the same: not long enough.

Goodbyes became a ritual. I once resisted them, pretending that leaving didn't matter. Eventually, I learned that refusing those farewells just left holes. So I went through the motions; awkward last hangouts, addresses on notebook paper, promises to call or write. Within months, the calls fell off; within a year, names blurred into other towns and faces.

I remember one goodbye more clearly than most. I must have been around eleven, leaving Missouri for South Carolina. My best friend at the time, Matthew, came over the night before the movers arrived. We sat on the porch steps, kicking at the dirt, neither of us saying much. Finally, he asked, "So, you think we'll still be friends?"

I wanted to tell him, 'Yes, of course.' But even then, I knew better. "Yeah," I said anyway. We shook hands like grown men, which made us laugh, and then we went back to kicking the dirt in silence. By the time the moving truck pulled away the next morning, he was already a memory I was learning to pack away.

Not all upheaval came from orders. Some started at home. In South Carolina, my parents' marriage finally broke. Moves could be understood; orders had logic.

Divorce only cracked the ground beneath us and left us standing in the middle.

I remember the arguments in muffled voices behind closed doors, the silence at the dinner table afterward, the way my siblings and I looked at each other without asking questions we didn't want answered. By the time the papers were signed, I had learned a new kind of impermanence. Homes could be left behind, but so could families.

The Army always promised that no matter where we moved, we would move together. After South Carolina, I knew even that wasn't guaranteed.

Sometimes, moves weren't to a new duty station, but to be with family. For example, when my father deployed to Somalia once, maybe Cuba, we stayed in Buffalo, New York. That year, surrounded by relatives and longtime neighbors, I was the outsider, a southern-accented Army kid dropped for a single year. The cold was sharp, but it was nothing compared to the isolation of being temporary among the permanent.

Those endless moves, and the divorce layered on top of them, did something to me. They stripped away the illusion of permanence. Most kids grow up believing in roots, in the idea that their hometown will always be there, their childhood bedroom always waiting. I didn't have that. Home was wherever the Army sent us, and even that home was temporary. It made me restless, but it also made me adaptable. I could walk into a room full of strangers and figure out how to fit in. I could let go quickly when I had to. It was a matter of survival, and it would become one of the most important tools I carried into adulthood.

The night before a move, I'd stand in my empty room, trying to picture it as it was. By the time we unpacked elsewhere, those images faded; new walls, new smells, new shadows.

Looking back, I realize those moments shaped how I see the world. Moving taught me everything is temporary: friendships, neighborhoods, even the illusion of belonging. Divorce taught me the same thing about family. It was a lesson I didn't want. Still, it shaped me into who I am today.

By the time we got orders for Germany, my second time there, I told myself it would just be another move. But those last three years of high school were different. For the first time, I wasn't the only kid living out of boxes, practiced at quick friendships and long-distance goodbyes. I was surrounded by others who spoke the same unspoken language I'd carried my whole life.

On that base in Germany, for the first time, I felt like I was home.

Germany was supposed to be just another duty station. I braced myself for the usual cycle: boxes, awkward first days, cemented friendships. But the moment I walked through the gates of the high school on base, I realized it wasn't going to be the same.

For the first time, I wasn't the only kid who lived out of boxes or knew the hollow echo of an empty house. Here, everyone had lived the same life I had, packing up every two years, not bothering to decorate too much. Nobody needed explanations. For once, I wasn't "new." I was just another Army kid.

The school itself was small, close-knit in a way that felt electric. And yes, there were cliques, just like in the States. The jocks, the skaters, the gamers, the theater kids, they all staked out their corners. But unlike the schools back home, the lines weren't as sharp. You could sit with the athletes at lunch and still catch a late-night gaming session with the nerds, then head to the skate park the next afternoon without anyone acting like you were betraying them. The cliques were there, but the walls were more like chain-link fences you could step through whenever you wanted.

My world expanded quickly. I fell in with a mix, guys who skated, played ball, and spent hours on video games when the weather turned. At lunch, we'd gather in the same spot, swapping burned CDs and inside jokes. Some of my friends had lived in Japan before Germany, others in Italy, and a few in Alaska. We traded stories like currency, not to compete, but to prove we understood. The common denominator was that none of us was permanent. That awareness made friendships burn brighter. We lived like we didn't have time to waste.

But my senior year, I met Brandon, and that changed everything. He wasn't like the other kids I knew. For one, he was homeschooled; his mom ran his education while his dad served in the Army. When I first went over to their house, it felt different from any military family I'd been around. There was a warmth there, a steadiness I hadn't realized I was missing. His mom fussed over me like I was one of her own, making sure I'd eaten enough, asking about school in a way that felt more like real interest than small talk. His dad carried himself with the calm authority of a soldier, but there was humor under it, the kind that came out when the uniform came off.

Before long, I was at their house more than my own. We'd spend afternoons in Brandon's room, games running on the console while his mom brought in snacks. Sometimes his dad would step in, leaning against the doorframe, and toss us a story about training or deployment that sounded half like a warning and half like advice. I listened closely.

What struck me most was how easily they folded me into their family. There was no sense of being temporary, no clock ticking down the days until we'd have to say goodbye. They just accepted me. I became, in a way, their "adopted" kid. For someone who had spent his whole life as an outsider, drifting from one group to another, that kind of unconditional belonging meant everything.

That bond carried forward long after Germany. They showed up for my high school graduation, proud as if I were their own. Years later, they were there for my last walk at the Tomb, standing quietly in the crowd, steady in a way only family could be. After my first deployment, it was Brandon's family I found myself talking to, sorting through the weight I couldn't always share with others. They were there for the birth of my kids, and even for my wedding to my second wife. Every major milestone of my life, they've been a constant thread, something rare and precious for someone like me, whose whole life had been a string of goodbyes.

Looking back, I realize Germany wasn't just about finding friends at school or skating downtown. It was about finding permanence in a world I'd believed was built on impermanence. Brandon and his family gave me that. They showed me what it felt like to belong not just to a group, but to a family that chose me as much as I chose them.

Life on base and life off base were still two different worlds. On base, everything was orderly, uniform lawns, speed limits strictly enforced by MPs, the unspoken hierarchy of ranks filtering down even to the kids. Off base, it was freedom: cobblestone streets, graffiti tucked in alleyways, trains that could take you across the border for the price of a movie ticket. I straddled both, comfortable in each but never fully one or the other. Maybe that was the point.

The strongest memory from those years is the stability, not from permanence, but from being among people who shared my impermanence. Nobody saw me as temporary. For the first time, I was part of a world in constant motion, just like me.

Those last three years of high school in Germany gave me something I had never had before: a kind of home. Not in the sense of geography, my "home" was still just another place stamped on orders, but in the sense of belonging. For once, I wasn't the odd one out. For once, I felt steady, even if the ground beneath me could shift again at any time.

But stability never lasts long in an Army life. Graduation came, and with it, the question that had been hovering over me for years: what next? For some of my classmates, the answer was college. For others, it was following their parents back to the States for yet another move, another new start. For me, the answer had been forming in the background for years, sharpened by the legacy of my family and the shadow of 9/11. I didn't just want to move again—I wanted to choose where I went, to step fully into the world that had shaped me.

That decision carried me across an ocean, from the cobblestone streets of Europe back to the States, and eventually into a set of orders that would change my life forever. My first duty station was the 3rd U.S. Infantry Regiment, also known as "The Old Guard." At the time, I couldn't have known that this assignment, something sparked by a simple question, would set me on the path to the Tomb of the Unknown Soldier.

Chapter 2 – The Path to the Tomb

In February 2007, I arrived at Fort Myer, home of the 3rd U.S. Infantry Regiment, "The Old Guard." The winter air stung as I stepped from the car, duffel bag over my shoulder. My stomach twisted with apprehension; every uncertain step felt heavier. Basic training had taught me to be a soldier, but nothing prepared me for what waited here.

I was lucky that my father lived in the area. He met me after graduation and drove me up to the post. That ride brought a small, grateful relief—a sliver of normalcy when I was desperate for reassurance. After weeks of drill sergeants barking me down and barracks stripped of comfort, sinking into the passenger seat of his car almost felt safe, a reminder that I hadn't been entirely changed. We didn't talk much; my father was a man of silence, but the comfort of his presence steadied me, and the shared quiet calmed the turmoil tightening in my chest. When we pulled up to the gates of Fort Myer, anxiety flickered with awe: I was entering a world nothing in my past could prepare me for.

Check-in happened late at night. Soldiers sat at the desk of the battalion on what's referred to as battalion staff duty. They seemed bored but alert when we walked in, curiosity engaged on their face, wondering who we were. My father and I walked up to the desk, where the soldiers' looks changed from boredom to something else.

Something strange happened then, something I still smile about. The unit mistook my father for the incoming Command Sergeant Major. His presence, his bearing, his confidence; it fit the part, even if he wasn't the man they expected. They welcomed us both, treating me and another young soldier as the new arrivals and my father as though he were stepping into a position of authority. They weren't wrong about us being new, but they were very wrong about him. The mistake worked in my favor, though. Instead of being thrown straight into work, they allowed me to leave with my father to enjoy a four-day pass before officially reporting on Tuesday.

Those few days felt like stolen time, fleeting and precious. My wife at the time had driven from my graduation, our entire life jammed into a tiny Dodge Neon. She met me at my father's house; the sight of her car trunk and backseat packed made my throat tighten with both hope and fear. It wasn't much, but in those boxes and bags was everything we owned, and seeing her reminded me just how raw and new our beginning was. We were both young and untested, carrying the fragile weight of a new marriage and the uncertainty of Army life, hoping somehow that our togetherness would see us through.

The contrast between basic training and the Old Guard was immediate. In basic, everything was about warfighting: weapons qualifications, field exercises, rucksacks, and drills that rehearsed combat over and over. Uniform standards mattered, but they were secondary to battlefield readiness and effectiveness. Here, the emphasis shifted. Drill and ceremony weren't just something to pass in formation—they were the centerpiece. The precision of a pivot, the exactness of a rifle movement, the sharpness of a salute. Those things mattered as much as, if not more than, the skills I had been taught in basic. At first, it felt strange, almost disorienting, like I had stepped into a different Army altogether. But it didn't take long to realize that this was its own kind of battlefield. The enemy wasn't another soldier; it was imperfection.

Living near Washington, D.C., added another layer of strangeness. I had never been in a city so crowded, so alive with movement. The hum of traffic, the constant flow of people, the rush of the Metro, this was nothing like the posts or small towns I had grown up in. Most people traveled by subway, something I had never experienced until then. The city seemed endless, with monuments and museums, history layered on every block. You could live there a lifetime and never see it all. For someone who had moved constantly, even the city itself felt transient, as though it belonged more to the world than to the people living in it.

Emotionally, I was torn between pride and frustration. Pride, because I had survived basic, earned a spot in one of the most prestigious Army units, and lived at the doorstep of history. I felt frustrated because I wanted to serve on the front lines. I hadn't expected The Old Guard. Meanwhile, as a newlywed, I felt the weight of responsibility settling on my shoulders. D.C.'s cost of living was suffocating, and even with BAH, my private's paycheck barely kept us afloat. Survival sometimes meant anxiety—stretching every dollar, worrying if we'd make rent. The constant pressure strained my marriage, compounding everything I felt in uniform.

Despite all that, I knew I was standing on the edge of something important. The soldiers I saw around me carried themselves differently. Razor-sharp uniforms, shoes polished until you could see your reflection, movements rehearsed until they looked effortless. This wasn't the Army most people saw. This was the Army on display, the Army of ceremony and tradition. I didn't understand yet how I fit into it, but I knew one thing: I had been given the chance to prove myself, and whatever doubts I carried, I wasn't going to waste it.

The first real step in the Old Guard was the Regimental Orientation Program (ROP). Every new soldier went through it, a three-week program, Monday through Friday. While most of the unit was off at their companies, we were pulled aside to be retrained and shaped into the exact image the Old Guard demanded.

ROP wasn't about advanced techniques or anything flashy. We didn't spin rifles or perform tricks. Everything was stripped back to the absolute basics: how to stand at parade rest with a weapon, how to salute, how to move through the manual of arms with precision. Port arms, order arms, present arms, simple movements that any soldier learned in basic training, but here they were elevated into something else. Every detail mattered. The angle of the rifle, the way your hand gripped the stock, the timing of your salute; all of it had to be exact, not just approximate.

We practiced over and over until muscle memory took over. If one soldier was off by a fraction, the whole formation looked sloppy. That was unacceptable in the Old Guard, where the public's eyes were always on us. I quickly realized this was a different Army than the one I had been introduced to in basic training. Basic taught me to fight, to move, to survive. ROP taught me to represent the Army itself before the nation and the families of the fallen. It wasn't about combat—it was about ceremony, reverence, and precision.

Flags were another major part of ROP. We learned how to fold the American flag with absolute consistency, each fold crisp, each movement deliberate. It wasn't just a training exercise. These flags were the ones that would be handed to grieving families at funerals in Arlington. We weren't just folding fabric. We were folding memory, sacrifice, the weight of a life given in service. That awareness crept into us slowly, lesson by lesson, until the act felt sacred.

Inspections became a daily routine. Uniforms were checked against a micrometer, measured down to the thirty-second of an inch. Shoes were inspected for shine, brass for alignment, and hair for length. At the time, I thought those inspections were intense. Later, I would learn the Tomb pushed the same process to the sixty-fourth of an inch, but in ROP, the scrutiny was already enough to set us apart from the rest of the Army. It gave me a false sense of confidence that would come back to haunt me when I began Tomb training. I walked out of ROP thinking I understood uniforms, only to discover later that I had barely scratched the surface.

Being named an honor graduate of my ROP class felt oddly easy. I wasn't more talented. I just cared more, I worked harder. As a brand-new private, still shaped by basic training, I clung to a steady rhythm: follow orders, ask when unsure, put in the effort. When an instructor corrected me, I listened; when I was confused, I spoke up, heart pounding but determined. I watched my peers tense up, afraid to be noticed, haunted by the old Army belief that questions exposed weakness or brought trouble. I felt that fear too, but I pushed through. For me, asking questions proved I wanted to get it right. That stubborn courage set me apart.

There wasn't much in the way of peer relationships during ROP. Everyone was focused on surviving the three weeks, completing the drills, and passing inspections. The one exception was a familiar face: one of my old battle buddies from basic training. He had decided, at the last minute, to come to the Old Guard as well. We competed for honor grad, quietly trying to outdo each other. I remember telling him one afternoon that I was curious about the Tomb of the Unknown Soldier. We had heard a brief pitch about it back in our basic training when the Old Guard recruiters visited. Something about it stuck with me, and I admitted that I was thinking about volunteering. He laughed outright. "You'll never make it," he told me. The words stung, but they also stuck. If anything, his doubt hardened my resolve.

Looking back, ROP was my first real taste of Old Guard precision. It wasn't hard compared to what would come later, but it introduced me to the culture of scrutiny, which demanded standards that left no room for sloppiness. It was similar to cleaning a weapon in basic training: you could think it was spotless, but under inspection, someone would find carbon hidden in a corner. In ROP, they applied that same kind of scrutiny to uniforms, posture, marching, and grooming standards.

What I didn't realize was how much this prepared me for the Tomb. ROP taught that details matter and perfection is a continual pursuit. The standard was higher than anything I knew, but it was only the start. When I finished ROP, I didn't go through any complicated reassignments. I was already assigned to Charlie Company when I checked in from basic training, so after graduation from orientation, I simply reported back to begin work. My platoon assignment was the Escort Platoon, one of the three line platoons that rotated through the funeral missions in Arlington National Cemetery.

Escort Platoon's role was straightforward but essential. We led the horse-drawn caisson carrying the fallen, marching ahead of the team and setting the pace. Once at the gravesite, we formed up and stood in silence while the ceremony unfolded. Rifle Platoon performed the three volleys that echoed across the headstones, and Casket Platoon carried the weight of the fallen, unloading the casket, folding the flag, and placing it into the arms of a grieving family member. Our part was quieter, less direct with the family, but it was no less important. We were there to guide the fallen on the last steps of their journey.

Life in the Escort Platoon fell into a rhythm quickly. Each day began with physical training from 0630 to 0800. We ran in formation through the streets of Fort Myer, boots striking pavement in cadence, songs carrying through the morning air. After PT came breakfast, usually a rushed affair in the dining facility, before we returned to the company area. Uniform inspections were held daily, about fifteen minutes before we stepped off for a mission. Team leaders checked every detail of our dress blues. The press of the trousers, the shine of the shoes, the placement of ribbons and medals. It wasn't yet Tomb standards, but it was still meticulous compared to what most soldiers in the Army experienced.

We kept our uniforms in lockers in an open-bay room, rows of them lined up against the walls. After inspections, we dressed, tightened our ranks, and prepared for the day's ceremonies. If we were not on "primary week", the week our platoon handled the majority of funerals, we drilled. Rehearsal after rehearsal, marching, turning, correcting cadence until it became automatic. Sometimes we filled in for additional ceremonies; retirements, changes of command, or special events that required Old Guard soldiers to stand as the Army's face to the public. There was always something on the schedule.

I still remember my first escort mission. Surprisingly, I wasn't nervous—just focused, shielded by the training and calm leadership of my platoon. I knew my role: set the pace, maintain formation, hold bearing. Unlike the men of Casket Platoon, who stood just feet from grieving families, our distance in the Escort Platoon offered relief at first. I could avoid their eyes, their pain. Instead, I concentrated on every step, feeling the drumbeat of boots, my breath heavy in the crisp air, while the chaplain's voice echoed off the silent headstones. We did five funerals a day. The routine never softened the sorrow; each funeral pressed down with its own new weight. But in those days, I barely grasped the depth of what I carried.

The duality of soldier life was obvious even then. In the cemetery, we carried ourselves with absolute seriousness, every step measured, every movement deliberate. Back at the barracks, soldiers were soldiers again—rowdy, loud, laughing, blowing off steam in ways only young infantrymen can. I didn't live in the barracks myself; I was married and living off base with my wife. That life was different. Our days outside of duty were spent like any young couple trying to get by with limited money. We cooked simple meals, walked the base, or took advantage of Washington, D.C.'s free sites. The National Mall, monuments, and museums that charged nothing but still offered the richness of history and culture. We didn't have much, but we had the city, and sometimes that was enough.

Though we shared missions across the cemetery, the three platoons —Escort, Rifle, and Casket —didn't interact much day to day. Our roles were distinct, our training separate. There were friendly rivalries, of course. PT often turned competitive, with platoons or even companies pushing to outdo each other. Who could run farther in cadence, who looked sharper in formation, who carried out their duties with the most precision? But for me, the time in Charlie Company was short-lived. I hadn't been there long enough to dive fully into the culture or rivalry before my path shifted again.

Still, the Escort Platoon left its mark. The precision of those missions, the discipline of daily inspections, the solemnity of funerals. It was another step in preparing me for what lay ahead. At the time, I couldn't know that in a matter of weeks, I would trade the rhythm of funeral honors for the silence of the Tomb, stepping into a duty that demanded more than I could yet imagine.

My first week on "primary" with Escort Platoon went more smoothly than I expected. By then, the drills and rehearsals had prepared me sufficiently, and my leadership ensured I understood my place in the formation. What struck me most wasn't the mechanics of the ceremonies—it was the families. Each day, time in and time out, I watched them arrive at the cemetery to bury their loved ones. Some were quiet, moving with a kind of practiced solemnity. Others wept openly, the grief fresh and raw. Standing in formation, leading the caisson, I felt the rhythm of their sorrow settle into me. It wasn't loud, it wasn't chaotic—it was serene, in its own way. Even as a new soldier, I understood that these ceremonies weren't about us. They were about creating a dignified final chapter for men and women who had worn the uniform before us. That week left an impression I would never forget.

It was during that rotation that the question slipped out. Simple, almost casual, but life-changing. I had heard bits and pieces about the Tomb of the Unknown Soldier from other soldiers. Not in the barracks, since I lived off-post with my wife, but during conversations at work. The whispers came in between missions, in the company area, or while waiting to step off for ceremonies. Most of what I heard was about how brutal the training was or how many guys had gone down there only to fail and get sent back. Some called it "hell," a place that stripped soldiers bare. Others focused on the badge itself, the Tomb Guard Identification Badge, calling it the least-awarded badge in the entire U.S. military. That phrase stuck with me: *the least-awarded badge.* It carried a gravity I couldn't shake.

When Sergeant Justin Bickett, Badge Number 533, showed up at Charlie Company that week, the opportunity presented itself. He looked sharp, carried himself with a presence I hadn't seen before. And what struck me even more was how our First Sergeant treated him. The First Sergeant didn't tower over him like he would with any other junior NCO. He spoke to him almost like an equal. That respect wasn't about rank. It was about the badge on Bickett's chest.
I couldn't help myself. When the briefing ended, I asked. My voice was steady, though I didn't think the question would lead anywhere. "Sergeant, how does training at the Tomb work? How long does it usually take?"

Bickett didn't hesitate; he explained it plainly. Once you're sent to the Tomb, that becomes your only mission. Funeral details, changes of command, and other Old Guard ceremonies are left behind. The Tomb consumes everything. New guys spend their duty rotation learning the basics. Then they train at night, after the cemetery gates close. They walk the plaza under supervision until they prove they're ready. The average candidate took six to nine months to earn the badge. Some took longer. Most never made it. The standards were unforgiving. Every detail mattered: uniforms, knowledge, movements, discipline. There was no margin for error. He didn't soften the truth, but neither did he embellish it. He told it like it was.

The number stuck with me. Six to nine months. That was the average. I didn't feel intimidated. If anything, I felt curious. Something inside me said, *I can endure that. I can handle six to nine months.*

My squad leader and team leader noticed my interest. Instead of brushing me off, they told me to bring it up with the First Sergeant. Their tone carried a kind of approval I hadn't expected. "You'd be a good candidate," one of them said. "You've already proven yourself in ROP, and you're picking things up fast."

The First Sergeant agreed. He spoke directly with Bickett about me, telling him I had graduated at the top of my class in ROP, scored high in basic training, and adjusted quickly to the regiment's standards. In his eyes, I was worth sending down to try. He didn't ask me if I wanted it. He just signed me up.

In the Army, we had a word for that: "voluntold." You didn't exactly volunteer, but you didn't say no, either. You got chosen. That was how I ended up with orders for temporary duty at the Tomb of the Unknown Soldier.

Looking back, I still believe it was more than a coincidence. At the time, it felt like curiosity and timing. But as I've gotten older, I see it differently. My faith has always shaped how I understand moments like that. I believe I asked the question because I was curious, but I believe fate had already chosen me for the Tomb. That simple question, that casual conversation, was the doorway to something bigger, something I couldn't see yet as a young private. Fate was already moving me toward a path I never could have imagined.

That path became real only weeks later, when I made my first visit to the Tomb of the Unknown Soldier as a candidate. It was May of 2007, and the air still carried the coolness of spring. The sun was just cresting over Washington, D.C., washing the skyline in gold and throwing long shadows across the marble hills of Arlington. The timing felt deliberate, as if fate itself had arranged the scene to mark my first steps into this new world.

We were escorted onto the plaza before the cemetery opened to the public. The silence struck me immediately, heavier than anything I'd felt before. Even among the small group of candidates, no one spoke. The marble seemed to demand it. The only sounds were the faint shuffle of shoes on stone and the distant calls of birds breaking the morning calm.

Then I saw him. The morning BOLO—the guard posted an hour before the cemetery opened. He was already on the mat, dressed in full blues, moving with absolute precision. His steel-tipped shoes struck the marble in a rhythm that felt eternal. *Click. Click. Click.* Each step was deliberate, each pause exact, every turn a study in discipline. His rifle shifted only when required, cradled as if it had always belonged there. Watching him, I felt the weight of tradition settle into my chest. This was no rehearsal. This was living history, carried forward in silence and precision.

Awe washed over me, followed quickly by nerves. My heart raced, though I forced myself to stand steady. This was far removed from Charlie Company, far different than escorting a caisson or standing at a graveside. It wasn't about families or dignitaries. It was about the Unknowns themselves. My mind whispered, *This is different.*

Sergeant Bickett's voice broke through the silence. He explained the daily regimen of the Tomb: inspections that caught every imperfection, rotations that kept the watch unbroken, knowledge that had to be memorized line by line, word for word. His tone carried the same weight as the BOLO's cadence—measured, deliberate, final. He didn't need to dramatize anything; the proof walked in front of us.

Finally, we were led downstairs, beneath the Memorial Amphitheater, into the quarters. The descent felt symbolic, like leaving the visible world of ceremonies for the hidden crucible where Sentinels were forged.

The air changed as soon as we stepped inside. It smelled of starch, polish, leather, and sweat; a mixture I'd come to associate forever with discipline. The quarters were not large, but every inch was used with precision. The racks were set with the tomb guards' gear ready for a walk and uniforms hanging perfectly pressed. Shoes, belts, bayonets, and scabbards rested in exact order. Tables and workbenches bore the marks of constant labor, irons and polish standing ready.

The atmosphere was heavy, but in a different way than the plaza above. Here, it wasn't the silence of marble or history. Instead, it was the silence of tension. The *new guys*, those still in training, barely spoke. They didn't even look at us. Eyes stayed down. Movements were sharp and efficient. They carried themselves with the haunted awareness of men under constant scrutiny, as if any word or glance might betray weakness. To me, they seemed like shadows—present, moving, but not daring to assert themselves.

The badge holders were different. They were the ones who spoke, asking us where we were from, what had brought us down here, why we wanted to try. Their questions weren't small talk. They wanted to know if our motivations were genuine. Their tone carried curiosity, but also judgment. They had all been "new guys" once. They knew how brutal the process was, and they knew most who stood where I stood would never finish it. Their words probed not just our answers but our resolve.

I remember feeling the pressure of those conversations, the unspoken test in every question. It wasn't enough to say, *I'm here because I want to be.* They wanted to hear if something deeper had brought you down. Something beyond curiosity. Something that could sustain you when everything in you wanted to quit. In those moments, I reflected on what drove me. The respect for history and tradition, the commitment to honor those who came before me, and the dedication to becoming a part of something larger than myself. It was this deeper motivation that I held onto, a reminder of why I started and what I hoped to achieve. Developing and holding onto such a motivation could help any new soldier navigate the challenges ahead and persevere when times get tough.

Even in those first moments, I understood that the Tomb was more than a duty—it was a separation. The plaza above was what the world saw: marble, uniforms, cadence. But here in the quarters, behind the locked doors and silence, was where the real work happened. Where men were broken down, rebuilt, and either forged into Sentinels or discarded.

Standing there, I felt the nerves twist in my stomach again. I hadn't taken a step on the mat yet, but I knew: I had entered something entirely different than anything I had ever known. This wasn't just a duty station. It was a crucible.

The Tomb's place inside the Old Guard made that distinction even clearer. On paper, I was assigned to Echo Company. The company that housed the regiment's specialty platoons. Echo was already different from the line companies like Charlie or Delta. Where they carried the bulk of funeral honors and infantry training, Echo handled missions that demanded a different kind of precision.

The Presidential Salute Battery thundered cannons for state ceremonies. The U.S. Army Drill Team spun and snapped rifles with flawless synchronization to showcase the Army's discipline. The Caisson Platoon guided horse-drawn carriages carrying the fallen through Arlington's roads, the steady clip of hooves marking their solemn pace. The Continental Color Guard bore the flags of our nation's history in parades and ceremonies that stretched from D.C. to distant posts.

Each of those platoons had its own discipline and its own pride. But even among them, the Tomb stood apart. The Drill Team had audiences. The Caisson Platoon had schedules. The Salute Battery fired when the ceremonies were called. The Tomb, by contrast, never stopped. Day or night, storm or summer heat, the mat was never empty. Since 1926, through wars, hurricanes, blizzards, and even 9/11, the watch had never broken. That unbroken vigil gave the Tomb a gravity even the other specialties respected.

Later, during my time, the specialty platoons were reorganized under Headquarters Company. The paperwork changed, the reporting chains shifted, but none of that touched what mattered. The Tomb wasn't defined by its place on an organizational chart. Its identity came from the silence of the plaza and the creed etched into every Sentinel who walked there.

For me, the difference was obvious the moment I set foot in the quarters. Escort Platoon had inspections, schedules, and rehearsals, but there was still room for chatter, for laughter, for the ordinary rhythm of soldiers. Down at the Tomb, it was silence, discipline, and weight. Even away from the plaza, you could feel the presence of the Unknowns above you.

That was the divide I began to recognize then—the difference between ceremonial and sacred. Other platoons required polish. The Tomb demanded devotion. One could be practiced. The other had to be lived.

The difference between ceremonial and sacred was already sinking in, but I had only begun to grasp the weight of what I was walking into. Looking back now, I can still feel that mix of emotions from those early days as a candidate. Hope that I could prove myself, anxiety that I might not measure up, and the gnawing awareness that I was stepping into something far larger than I understood.

There were seventeen of us who started the process around that time, each one carrying our own reasons for being there. Some came out of curiosity, some because they wanted the respect that came with the badge, and a few because they thought it might be easier than deploying with a line unit. The Tomb had a way of exposing those motives quickly. It didn't matter why you came—it mattered whether you could endure. And most couldn't.

Even then, I knew the numbers. The failure rate hovered around ninety-five percent. Out of the seventeen of us who walked into those quarters as fresh candidates, only a handful would ever make it out the other side with a badge pinned to their chest. Some would quit. Others would be sent back to their companies after failing one test too many. A few would make progress but stall out, the standard proving too steep. It was never about talent or strength. It was about patience, persistence, and resilience under constant pressure.

In those first days, standing on the plaza and walking through the quarters, I began to realize that everything at the Tomb stripped you down to your core. The marble silence didn't care about your background, your pride, or your reasons. It cared only about whether you could walk twenty-one steps without flaw, stand in storms without moving, memorize pages of knowledge until they were etched into your brain, and polish your uniform until no gig could be found. It was a crucible designed to break you—and if you endured, to remake you.

Hope was there, yes, but so was fear. Not the fear of combat. I hadn't seen that yet. This was the fear of failure. The fear of not being enough. The Tomb demanded perfection. I had no illusions about how far I was from perfect. I carried doubts every time I thought about the tests ahead of me. Could I memorize that much? Could I keep my composure under that kind of scrutiny? Could I live up to the badge holders, those whose presence commanded respect even from First Sergeants?

At the same time, a quiet determination began to take root. If the standard were perfection, then I would chase it. If the odds were stacked against me, then I would outlast them. I didn't know how yet. I didn't know what it would cost me. But I knew I wasn't going to quit.

The Tomb had already shown me enough to understand that this wasn't a place where shortcuts survived. It wasn't about getting by—it was about transformation. And that transformation was about to begin in earnest.

For all the silence of those first days—the BOLO pacing the mat, the hushed quarters, the quiet weight of marble and history—I knew what was coming would not be quiet. Training would test us in every way: long nights of memorization, endless inspections, the sting of failure, the grind of discipline. Resilience would become more than a word; it would become a matter of survival.

Seventeen of us had walked in together. By the end, only a few would remain.

The Tomb was waiting to see which one I would be.

Next came TDY. The fourteen-day trial by fire that would decide if I had even the potential to stand the eternal watch.

Chapter 3 – Trial by Fire

My time at the Tomb began on TDY, which stands for temporary duty. Every new soldier started there, fourteen days on trial. It was a simple system: in those two weeks, you either proved you had the potential to become a Tomb Guard, or you were sent back to your company. TDY was the gatekeeper, and for good reason. The Tomb had no use for soldiers who weren't ready to be broken down and rebuilt.

The first night was quiet. New guys didn't say much. In fact, they barely spoke at all, even when we were sitting in the same room. They didn't look at us long, didn't waste time with small talk. If they were still in training, their focus was survival. If they had already earned the badge, their focus was on maintaining perfection. Either way, they weren't about to waste energy on newcomers who might not last the week. Badge holders, on the other hand, asked the real questions: *Why are you here? Do you think you have what it takes?* Their tone wasn't cruel, just direct, as if they wanted to measure your motivation before they invested their time in you.

The quarters themselves felt different than anything I'd experienced in the Army so far. Beneath the Memorial Amphitheater, the atmosphere was tighter, heavier. Upstairs, tourists would one day crowd behind the chains to watch the guard change, but downstairs, there were no crowds, no distractions. Just the pressure of the job and the silence of men preparing for it.

Days in TDY had their own rhythm. We reported around 0500 and didn't leave until roughly 1700. Unlike relief-assigned Sentinels, we didn't stay overnight yet. We weren't permanent. We were temporary guests, candidates being tested. Every day felt like borrowed time.

Mornings began with uniform prep and small corrections. If you were lucky, a badge holder or a more senior new guy would point out where you were already failing. "That ribbon's crooked." "Your seam's off." "Do it again." The rest of the day was consumed by knowledge recitations, endless repetitions of facts and details until they blurred together. Evenings stretched long, with badge holders pulling us onto the quiet plaza after the cemetery closed, drilling us in silence under the dim lights.

But TDY wasn't only about reciting or marching. It was about proving you could embrace the grind.

One of the first things handed to us was a scabbard—an old, dull green one from Vietnam, scarred by time and covered in rust and pitting. It was useless in its current condition, but that was the point. Stripping it down, sanding away the pits, pulling apart the metal fittings, repainting the wood black, reassembling and shining it—it wasn't busywork. It was a test of patience. Could you take something broken and bring it to standard? Could you focus for hours on details so small that most people would never notice them?

Shoes were the same. They gave us old pairs, scarred and worn, and told us to strip them down to bare leather. We dyed them, polished them, and worked them until our fingers ached. No one in TDY ever achieved a true mirror finish. That was beyond our reach at that stage. But the goal wasn't to produce perfection in two weeks. It was to prove you had the discipline to chase it, to show that you were willing to grind away at something that looked impossible.

We carried everything in and out by hand every day. Unlike assigned Sentinels, we didn't have lockers. That meant lugging multiple uniforms, raincoats, PT gear, and dress shoes back and forth daily, always under the risk of inspection. It was exhausting, and that was the point. The Tomb wasn't interested in making your life easier. It was interesting to find out if you could handle inconvenience without complaint, if you could maintain standards while tired, overloaded, and frustrated.

Recitation was where most cracked. Standing in the quarters, binder closed, you would speak the words of the Sentinel's Creed, the poems, and the history of the Unknowns. Ten errors were allowed, no more. You made too many mistakes, and you were cut. The silence after a failure was worse than being yelled at. Badge holders rarely raised their voices. They didn't need to. The weight of their silence told you everything. You weren't good enough yet.

Outside performance was its own crucible. Heel clicks, facing movements, weapon carries—every detail was dissected. Ten gigs were allowed. No major gigs allowed. Drop the weapon, carry it wrong, miss a command—and you were done. The plaza was unforgiving, even in training. The sound of steels striking stone echoed louder when you knew each step was being judged.

The hardest part wasn't the knowledge, the uniform, or even the plaza. It was the waiting. You waited for inspections. You waited for badge holders to call you. You waited for corrections. And in that waiting, doubt crept in. Every stumble felt louder than it was. Every mistake made you wonder if you would even last the two weeks.

By the end of TDY, three of the seventeen men I had started with were gone. They didn't pack up lockers, because none of us had them yet. They just stopped showing up. One day, they were beside us, sweating through recitations and working on shoes and scabbards, and the next, they weren't. No explanations. No goodbyes. The Tomb had moved on without them.

When the fourteen days ended, the rest of us stood waiting for our next step. TDY was over. We had survived the trial, but survival was only the beginning. Orders were read out, assigning us to our reliefs—1st, 2nd, or 3rd—based on our height. Being assigned to a relief gave you a place to train and a group to belong to, but it didn't change your status. You were still a "new guy." You would remain a new guy until the day you passed your badge test. Whether that took one month or the full twelve. Until then, you carried the title, the scrutiny, and the constant pressure that came with it.

The binder was heavy in more ways than one. At first glance, the first seven pages seemed straightforward lines of text, dates, and facts. But once you started trying to internalize them, you realized they weren't just words; they were expectations.

The Sentinel's Creed came first, and every line carried weight. I can still remember whispering it over and over until the words blurred in my mind:

"My dedication to this sacred duty is total and wholehearted. In the responsibility bestowed on me never will I falter."

Those weren't just lines to memorize. You felt them pressing down on you in the quarters. You stood there, binder closed, voice low but firm, repeating until your throat was dry. A badge holder would stand before you, silent, waiting for a slip. Ten errors or fewer, they'd let you keep going. But when you stumbled—when you froze on a line you'd said a hundred times—they didn't yell. They just stared at you, unreadable. That silence hit harder than any shouting.

I remember one night vividly. I was halfway through reciting the details of the four crypts, World War I beneath the Tomb itself, World War II, Korea, and Vietnam on the rear side, when my mind went blank. Nothing. Just a wall of silence in my head. Seconds felt like hours. I tried to recover, to skip forward, but I tripped again. Finally, the badge holder leaned in slightly and said, flatly, "Start over."

No anger. No explanation. Just those two words.

I went back to the beginning, voice cracking. By the end of that recitation, sweat was running down my back like I had just finished PT. It wasn't the heat, it was the pressure. That night, lying awake, I repeated the Creed and the crypt details until I fell asleep. It wasn't about not making mistakes anymore. It was about proving to myself that I wouldn't freeze again.

If knowledge tested your memory, the uniform tested your patience—and for me, it was the hardest part.

Every day revolved around preparing that uniform, and it consumed hours upon hours.

The blouse, pants, and hat alone could take anywhere from one to ninety minutes of work. The blouse had to be pressed so that not a single ripple showed under the harsh eyes of a badge holder. Pants had to have creases sharp enough to cut paper, pressed and re-pressed until they looked almost unnatural in their perfection. Medals, awards, and citations had to be measured with a micrometer, down to the tiniest fraction of an inch. Nothing could be crooked. Nothing could be "close enough." Everything had to align exactly as the standard demanded.

But that was only the beginning. The bulk of my time, four to six hours a day, went into shining shoes. You stripped them down to bare leather, dyed them, layered polish, let it dry, buffed, repeated. Over and over, building up the surface until it reflected like glass. It was mind-numbing work, sitting there for hours, with the smell of polish and dye in the air, hands stained black, and a back aching from leaning over.

While waiting for the polish to dry, I'd turn to my scabbard. It had been issued to me dull green, relics from Vietnam-era gear, with metal that was pitted and rusted. I stripped the paint, scrubbed the rust, and polished the steel until every flaw was gone. Then it was repainted black and rebuilt, every piece shining, every edge perfect. It wasn't optional. It was expected. Just like the shoes, it became a daily ritual, one more reminder that nothing about the Tomb was casual.

I hated working on my uniform. It was my least favorite part of the job. I didn't have the natural patience some of the other guys did. For me, every hour at the ironing board or bent over those shoes was a fight against frustration. But I did it anyway. Because at the end of the day, the Tomb wasn't about me. It was bigger than me, bigger than any one Sentinel. My standard had to remain perfection. Not because I wanted to polish shoes for half the day, but because the Unknowns deserved nothing less.

The inspections themselves were brutal. We lined up in the quarters, silence hanging heavy in the air. You could smell the faint bite of starch from freshly pressed cloth, the lingering scent of shoe polish that never really left. Badge holders walked the line slowly, eyes sharp, noting every detail. They didn't need to say much; the weight of their presence was enough. A ribbon slightly off-center, a tie not perfectly flush, a scabbard with the faintest imperfection in its shine. Any of it could earn a gig. Seven were allowed at this stage, but in reality, every mistake felt like it might be the one to end you.

I nearly failed once. My tie had shifted just slightly, barely noticeable to me in the mirror. But to a badge holder, it stood out immediately. He marked it down without hesitation: "Gig." My heart sank. It was just one mistake, but it reminded me how unforgiving the standard was. You could spend six hours shining shoes and an hour pressing cloth, but if one thing slipped, that's all anyone would see.

That was the lesson: at the Tomb, nothing was hidden, and nothing was forgiven. The uniform wasn't about pride or appearance—it was about devotion. Every polished shoe, every flawless seam, was a silent promise to the Unknowns that their sacrifice would be honored with nothing less than perfection.

If knowledge tests the mind and uniforms test patience, outside performance tests the soul. For me, it quickly became my favorite part of training. Out there on the mat, I wasn't just polishing shoes or repeating pages from a binder. I was standing with the Unknowns. Every step, every click of my heels, brought me closer to the heart of what it meant to be a Sentinel.

At night, after the cemetery gates closed and silence returned, the atmosphere shifted. The lights of the Amphitheater would hum on, casting long, steady shadows across the plaza. The rails lining the Amphitheater stairs threw sharp lines across the marble, cutting the light into bands of shadow and glow. We called it the shadow line.

I loved walking it. Hour after hour, sometimes two or three at a time, I traced that shadow line in silence. The mat felt different at night. Without tourists or crowds, there were no whispers or camera clicks. Only the echo of my steels against the stone, the rhythm of my breath, and the sense that the Unknowns were closer somehow. The stillness of those hours wrapped around you, steadying your nerves, drawing you deeper into the duty.

Perfection was demanded in every motion. You couldn't just march—you had to glide. Each step had to flow as though your body weighed nothing at all, as though the rifle in your hands were an extension of your arm rather than ten pounds of steel and walnut. Any bounce in your step, any clunky movement, was a gig. It didn't matter if it was 0300 and the plaza was empty except for badge holders watching in silence. Perfection was the standard.

The rifle itself added to the challenge. We drilled constantly on how to carry it—port arms, shoulder arms, inspection arms—every angle exact, every movement sharp but controlled. Everyone knew the rule: dropping your weapon outside on the mat was an instant end to your chance. But here's the truth. During my entire time at the Tomb, I never once saw a rifle dropped outside. Close calls, yes. Fingers that almost slipped, spins that wobbled, grips that faltered. But no one ever let go. We all knew what it would mean, and the fear alone was enough to keep your hands locked like steel.

Downstairs, during inspections and drills, it was a different atmosphere. Weapons inspections required you to spin the rifle through intricate movements, stopping it on a dime, snapping it into place with perfect timing. In that cramped training space, rifles hit the floor more than once. It was expected to be part of the process of learning control. But upstairs, on the mat, it was unthinkable. The Unknowns demanded more.

For me, outside performance was never just about impressing badge holders. It was communion. Each step in the shadow line was a conversation with silence, with sacrifice, with history itself. I could feel the weight of the Unknowns with me, and that made me want to glide smoothly, click sharply, and carry steadily. I wasn't just training. I was practicing reverence.

That's why I came to love it. Knowledge was stressful. Uniforms frustrated me to no end. But outside performance—walking, turning, guarding—was where I felt closest to the reason I was there. It was where the Tomb stopped being an assignment and started becoming a sacred duty.

Then there was the drill every new guy dreaded: *Three Minutes, Go.*

It always began in the knowledge corner. A badge holder would glance at his watch, look up, and say the words that made your stomach drop: "Three minutes, go."

The stopwatch started instantly.

Chaos followed. You had exactly 180 seconds to strip off whatever you were wearing—PTs, ACUs, whatever—and change into full Class A dress blues. Blouse, trousers, white shirt, tie, hat, shoes fully laced and tied. In one hand, you had to be holding your ceremonial belt with the scabbard attached. In the other, gloves and glasses. Only then, standing back in the knowledge corner, did the stopwatch stop.

It sounds simple. Until you're living it. Fingers shook as buttons slipped, ties knotted unevenly, pants caught on boots. Sweat poured, even in cool weather. Shoes, the bane of every new guy, had to be laced perfectly and tied off. More than once, someone sprinted back with laces undone, only to fail on the spot.

Badge holders didn't need to yell. Their silence as they ticked off mistakes was worse. "Tie crooked. Shirt tail out. Wrong shoe laced. Fail."

The drill wasn't just about speed. It was about composure under pressure. It taught you preparation: laying out your uniform in order, rehearsing the sequence until it became instinct. It also reminded you that Tomb Guards never worked alone. That belt had to be bloused on by someone else. Even under a stopwatch, you relied on the man next to you.

And over all of it hung the weather. The Tomb never paused for heat, or cold, or rain. Training was no different.

In summer, the sun baked the mat until it radiated heat through your soles. The black leather of your shoes threatened to soften, and the wool of your uniform clung with sweat. You felt like the plaza itself was trying to cook you alive. In winter, the icy wind cut through every layer until it felt like knives against your skin. Rifles turned into blocks of ice in your hands. Snow gathered in your hat, froze on your lashes, stiffened in the creases of your sleeves. Rain seeped through every stitch, chilling you until your bones ached.

And yet, through it all, you moved—twenty-one steps, twenty-one seconds, twenty-one steps back. The Unknowns hadn't chosen their conditions, so neither did we.

It had been about two months since I first arrived at the Tomb, and up to that point I had only drilled, practiced, and walked the shadow line at night. That evening, I finally earned the chance to walk the plaza in front of the public for the first time.

The walk wasn't a full posting—not yet. It was the evening BOLO, the final walk of the day. Every morning at 0700, an hour before the cemetery opened to the public, a Sentinel stepped onto the mat in full dress blues for the morning BOLO, ensuring the Unknowns were never left alone. At closing, the same thing happened again. The last BOLO of the evening, an hour-long walk in dress blues that marked the end of the day before the gates shut at 1900. A guard change still occurred at the top of the hour, so if the BOLO was at 1900, the relief would conduct a full ceremonial change to mark the end of the day.

That was the posting I had been chosen for.

By then the plaza was mostly quiet. The evening crowd rarely exceeded twenty people, a scattering of visitors lingering as the sun faded behind the trees. Small as it was, to me it might as well have been thousands.

I earned that walk earlier in the day, the way every candidate earned anything at the Tomb—by outperforming another new guy. We had been grilled mercilessly on knowledge, every fact and detail demanded word-for-word. Later came the uniform inspections, seams and medals checked against measurements so exact it felt like they could see flaws invisible to the naked eye. That day, I held my ground. I recited cleanly, stood through the critiques, and when it was done, a badge holder looked at me in the knowledge corner and said three words.

"Three minutes. Go."

The words slammed into me like a shockwave. My chest tightened as adrenaline surged. I sprinted out of the knowledge corner, tearing back into the new man room. My hands shook as I yanked on the white shirt, buttoned the blouse, tied the tie. Shoes laced and knotted. Scabbard ready. Gloves and glasses in hand. My breath came fast and shallow, heart hammering so hard it drowned out thought. The badge holder stepped in, snapped the ceremonial belt around my waist, and leveled me with a steady look.

"Breathe," he said. "Focus on what you've been practicing these last two months."

I climbed the stairs and stepped out onto the plaza.

The world tilted. The evening air was cool, the marble still warm from the sun, but it felt like the whole plaza was alive with eyes. The crowd was small, yet their presence pressed in on me from behind the chains. My footsteps carried me forward, steels clapping against the stone, each strike echoing louder than it ever had in practice.

In my nerves, I miscounted. I walked one step too far onto the plaza. For a split second, my stomach dropped. But the badge holder adjusted with flawless precision, covering the mistake so seamlessly that no one beyond the rail would have noticed. That was the difference between us. I was still raw. He was a Sentinel.

The guard change unfolded: rifles exchanged, steps measured, every movement deliberate. My mind roared with reminders. Don't bounce. Don't drag. Keep the rifle steady. Count every step. When the change ended and the relief marched off, I was left alone.

For the next hour, I walked the mat. Twenty-one steps, twenty-one seconds, twenty-one steps back. Visitors trickled toward the gates, their voices fading. The plaza settled into stillness, leaving me with nothing but the cadence of my own movement and the silent presence of the Unknowns.

Somewhere in that rhythm, my nerves loosened. The long nights on the shadow line came back. The endless hours walking the faint divide of light and shadow cast by the amphitheater's lamps, practicing until my legs burned. Out here, it all began to take shape.

When the hour ended and I came back downstairs, the badge holders were waiting. They told me where I had faltered, where my alignment slipped. But one of them also gave me a nod.

"Your walk looked clean," he said. "Shadow line's paying off."

It wasn't perfection. It wasn't even close. But it was my first walk, and I hadn't broken. For the first time, I felt that the mat wasn't just something I practiced on—it owned me now.

That sense of ownership deepened in the nights that followed. When the cemetery gates closed and the last visitors faded into the dusk, the Tomb didn't sleep. The evening BOLO ended the day's public watch, but an hour later, another kind of guard took over.

That exchange was simple but sacred. The outgoing guard would say, "Post and orders, remain as directed." The incoming guard would respond, "Orders acknowledged." There were no salutes, no calls, no public ritual. Just a quiet passing of responsibility, the unbroken chain of vigilance continuing even when the world above had turned out the lights.

For about an hour after that exchange, the plaza belonged to all of us. New guys and badge holders alike would come up to drill in the glow of the amphitheater lights. We walked through movements endlessly—heel clicks ringing sharp against marble, facing movements as crisp as if our boots had edges, weapons carried steady as stone. Shadows from the railings stretched across the plaza like black bars, slicing the light into patterns that shifted as we moved. We trained until every motion blurred into muscle memory, the plaza echoing with steps that no tourist would ever see.

When the training ended, the rest went back downstairs. But the posted guard in ACUs stayed. That Sentinel kept the vigil through the night.

Night watch at the Tomb was different than anything during the day. There was no mat confining you to a measured strip of steps. Instead, the entire plaza was yours to walk. You could move to the far corners, down the stairs, along the chains that stretched below. The air carried a deeper stillness, as though the marble itself was holding its breath. Every step echoed louder, every pause seemed longer.

Guarding in ACUs at night didn't feel like a ceremony. It felt like keeping a vigil. It was you, the Unknowns, and the silence. No applause, no visitors, no distractions. Just the marble, the dark sky overhead, and the weight of history pressing in close. It was in those hours that you realized the standard didn't belong to the public. It belonged to the Unknowns. Day or night, summer heat or winter ice, alone or in front of a thousand people, the standard was always the same: perfection.

Preparation for Test 1 consumed days. Every uniform we owned had to be ready, but the reality was that most of us picked one to showcase. You never neglected the others, but you poured your soul into a single set, knowing that was the one the badge holders would tear apart under the microscope. For me, that meant hours of pressing the blouse and trousers, checking medals and citations, and shining shoes until I thought the leather might wear thin.

When the day came, the first hurdle was the waiting. I remember standing for nearly two hours in that cramped room, motionless, heart hammering in my chest, waiting for the badge holder to finally begin. Those two hours were worse than the test itself. In that silence, every mistake you thought you'd made replayed in your mind. Was the ribbon bar perfectly aligned? Did I miss a thread on the seam? Was there dust on the hat brim I hadn't caught?

When the inspection began, it felt like time stretched thin. The badge holder started at the top—hat, brim, brass, every stitch—and worked slowly downward. Nothing escaped his eyes. The inspection lasted thirty, maybe forty-five minutes, but it felt like hours. Every time he leaned in closer, I wondered if he had found the gig that would sink me.

Then came the outside performance. They posted me twice in the morning and twice again in the evening, giving the badge holders a chance to see if my precision carried onto the plaza. It wasn't a ceremonial guard change, but every step was judged as if it was. Each heel click echoed sharper than normal in my own ears, each facing movement felt heavier with consequence. I forced myself to breathe, to stay focused on what I had practiced. By the end of those short walks, I had no idea if I had passed or failed.

The last piece came at the end of the day: the knowledge test. By then, my body was tired, but this part almost felt like relief. Knowledge was drilled into us daily in the knowledge corner. Dozens of recitations and endless corrections. Sitting down to write those first seven pages word-for-word wasn't easy, but it was familiar. My hand cramped, but the words flowed. When I finished, I knew I had passed at least this piece.

Looking back, the details of Test 1 blur together with the others that followed. The structure was always the same—uniform, performance, knowledge—but the standards grew tighter each time. Still, this first test mattered. Passing it meant I wasn't just a "new guy" surviving TDY. I was moving forward. I was allowed to start walking BOLOs, to feel the mat beneath my feet for real. I hadn't earned the badge yet, but I was on the path, and for the first time, I believed I might make it.

Test 2 was the turning point where the Tomb truly began to separate those who had potential from those who only thought they did. Passing Test 1 gave you access to the mat in limited windows. Early morning at 0700, before the cemetery opened to the crowds, or the evening BOLO when most visitors had already gone home. The plaza was never empty, but in those hours, the weight of the public was lighter.

Test 2 changed that.

This was the test that cleared you for "back-to-back," and back-to-back meant exactly what it sounded like: every available guard shift during the day. It wasn't just one or two walks strung together. If you were posted for back-to-back, you lived on that mat. If the cemetery opened at 0800, you were posted at the top of the hour, relieved at the half, came back down, and went straight into prep for the next hour's walk. Then you were back up at 0900. Relieved at 0930. Back up at 1000. Relieved at 1030. Over and over, until the cemetery closed for the day.

It was relentless.

You didn't have time to catch your breath before you were being bloused up again and sent back onto the plaza. There was no drifting back into the quarters, no long reset to polish or regroup. You barely had time to grab water, check your uniform, maybe adjust a detail, before the next relief was already forming and you were stepping back out into the sun.

That first day of back-to-back I'll never forget. The morning air still held a trace of cool, but by late morning, the sun was hammering the marble. I felt it radiating through my shoes, soaking into the black wool of my trousers. The plaza doesn't give mercy. Every hour was the same sequence—twenty-one steps, twenty-one seconds, twenty-one steps back—yet each time it felt heavier. By mid-day, sweat was running down my back and pooling at my collar, but my cadence never changed. It couldn't.

What made back-to-back different wasn't just the repetition. It was the presence of the public. At 0800, maybe a handful of visitors watched. By 1100, the rails were lined shoulder to shoulder. School groups, veterans with canes, tourists with cameras. All staring, waiting for the change, waiting to see perfection. You couldn't think about fatigue. You couldn't think about the hours still ahead. All you could think about was the Unknowns, and the promise that your standard would remain perfection.

Walking back-to-back was the Tomb's way of proving whether you had endurance in your body, but more importantly, in your mind. Anyone could make one walk look sharp. But could you repeat it, hour after hour, with no loss of precision? Could you hold your weapon at the exact same angle at 0800 and at 1700, even when your arms were screaming? Could you click your heels with the same sharpness in the final guard change of the day as you had in the first?

Not everyone could. The attrition proved it. By the end of Test 2, six more men were gone. Some failed the written portion, some crumbled under uniform inspections, but a few simply couldn't sustain the discipline required for back-to-back. Their standards slipped, and at the Tomb, a slip meant the end.

For me, back-to-back was both humbling and empowering. Humbling, because I knew my every move was being measured not just against myself, but against nearly a century of Sentinels who had done the same before me. Empowering, because for the first time, I felt the Tomb beginning to let me in. I wasn't just training anymore. I was walking in the heart of the watch, carrying the weight of the Unknowns for all to see.

By the end of Test 2, the numbers had thinned to almost nothing. Seventeen had started this path. Now, only three of us remained. The air in the quarters felt different after that test—emptier, heavier. Every correction, every failure, every late night of polishing or reciting knowledge had cut away at the group until only a few were left.

I was still standing, but it didn't feel like victory. It felt like a pause before the next storm. TDY was behind me. The first tests were behind me. But the hardest part, the Full Rotation and the Badge Test, was still ahead.

That night, binder in hand, I sat on the edge of the bunk and thought about what it would mean to finish, to finally shed the title of "new guy." The Tomb demanded more than just survival; it demanded transformation. And I knew the coming months would decide whether I had truly earned the right to walk the mat for the Unknowns, or whether I would be remembered as just another name that didn't make it through.

Chapter 4 – The Badge Earned

The week before the badge test carried its own kind of silence. The chatter in the quarters faded, replaced by the nervous rhythm of men lost in their own thoughts. Some buried themselves in their binders, lips moving quietly as they repeated lines of the Creed. Others hunched over their uniforms for hours, steam rising in clouds as irons hissed against fabric. A few tried to joke, but even the laughter sounded thin, like it was meant more for themselves than anyone else.

I barely slept. The smell of polish, starch, sweat, and coffee filled the room like a fog, clinging to everything. My hands were cracked from polish and heat. My eyes burned from the fluorescent lights that never seemed to go off. Every night blurred into the next, the hours measured not in sleep but in how many times I could press a crease, polish a shoe, or recite the same line without faltering.

Uniform prep became a ritual. An hour and a half on the blouse, pants, and hat, pressing and re-pressing until my fingers stung from burns. Four to six hours went into shoes, stripped and re-dyed, polished layer upon layer until they reflected like black glass. While they dried, I turned to the scabbard, rubbing away pits of rust until the metal gleamed, the leather repainted from faded green to a flawless black. Every piece demanded hours. Every piece demanded more.

Paranoia was constant. Medals and ribbons were measured with a micrometer, adjusted, and re-measured again minutes later. A tie that looked perfect under one light seemed crooked under another. More than once, I found myself fixing and unfixing the same detail, second-guessing if it had been straighter before I touched it. One night I nearly panicked over a medal bar that had shifted a fraction of an inch. It took nearly an hour to reset something no one else might have noticed—but at the Tomb, the smallest imperfection could decide your fate.

That was when the bottom almost fell out of me.

I was alone in the new man's room late, later than I should've been, surrounded by the glow of desk lamps and the soft, constant hum of the building. My blouse lay across my knees, the micrometer still in my hand. I had just found another tiny misalignment in a ribbon row and felt the familiar spark of frustration ignite into something rougher. The kind that tells you you're never going to get there. The kind that whispers you're not built for this.

I don't know how long I sat there, jaw tight, eyes burning, wishing I could be done with the whole thing. That's when Jeff Binek, Badge Number 563, stepped in. His TDY class had started after mine. He'd already passed. He didn't make an entrance, didn't clear his throat or bark a correction. He just saw me, saw the look on my face, and crossed the room.

"Let me see it," he said.

I handed him the blouse. He didn't lecture. He didn't posture. He ran the micrometer lightly across the bar, loosened a back clasp with quick, careful fingers, and nudged the rack a hair's breadth. He checked it again.

Then he set the blouse flat on the table and looked me in the eye.

"You've got what it takes," he said, voice quiet. "Finish what you started."

He helped me tighten the line of my tie, re-press a seam, and reset a tiny corner of ribbon backing that was pushing the row a whisper high. He didn't stay long. He wasn't there to rescue me. He was there to remind me what this place asked of us, and what we owed it in return. When he left, the room felt different. Not easier—never easier—but possible. His words carried me through that night and into the next.

The pressure wasn't just in the work—it was in the waiting. You told yourself over and over that the badge holders would see everything, even the flaw you hadn't found yet. And maybe they would. That fear kept your hands moving long after exhaustion begged you to stop

By the final night, there was nothing left to do but stare at the uniform and hope it was enough. The air in the quarters felt heavier than it ever had, as though it knew what was coming. I lay down with the binder still in my hand, reciting lines in the dark until the words blurred together.

The next morning would answer.

The morning of my badge test started like no other, though everything about it felt the same. That was the paradox: the plaza looked the same, the uniforms were the same, the drills were the same. But beneath it all, everything had changed. Today, my status as a "new guy" hung in the balance. By nightfall, I would either be a Sentinel or I would be sent back, carrying nothing but months of effort and failure.

The first trial of the day was the uniform inspection. I had spent days preparing one of my four uniforms for this moment. While all of them had to be ready, we each picked one to hold up under the microscope, and this was mine. I stood in the badge locker room, motionless, as the inspection began. The room was quiet except for the faint scratch of pen on paper as the two badge holders circled me like hawks, their eyes scanning every inch.

The micrometer moved across my uniform with agonizing slowness. They checked the spacing of my medals, the alignment of my belt buckle, and the razor's edge of each seam. From the hat on my head to the polished black shoes at my feet, nothing escaped their scrutiny. I could hear them whispering to each other, though I couldn't make out the words, only the sound of their voices and the occasional pause before more writing. Sweat trickled down my spine, but I didn't move a muscle. Over an hour had passed that way, every second stretching longer than the last.

Then came the outside performance. The part I had dreaded the least and yet feared the most. Unlike the uniform inspection, this wasn't a single event. That day, I walked *back-to-back*. Hour after hour, I stepped onto the plaza in full blues, performing the guard change and taking my place on the mat. Every twenty-one steps, every pause, every turn might be the moment they were grading me. But I didn't know when.

That uncertainty weighed heavier than the rifle in my hands. Every click of my heels could decide it. Every swing of the rifle might tip the balance. And all the while, the badge holders watched silently, hidden among the shadows, recording every flaw I couldn't see.

By this point in training, I had done roughly 750 official walks in full blues, not counting the countless hours of practice at night under the amphitheater lights. I knew the mat. I knew the rhythm. I had walked the shadow lines until my body moved as if pulled by the marble itself. In a way, I trusted myself here more than anywhere else. If there was one part of the badge test I was confident in, it was this.

But confidence didn't erase the nerves. Every time I marched down the mat, my mind screamed: Was that turn crisp enough? Did my timing drift? Did the rifle move too much on the shoulder? The mat was where I belonged, but it was also where I felt the full weight of what was at stake.

The day stretched on endlessly, one walk blending into the next. By evening, I was drained, my body aching, but still I kept the cadence. Still, I clicked my heels against the marble and willed myself not to falter. And still, I never knew which walk was *the one* that would be written into the record.

The final piece came back downstairs, in the badge locker room. A table had been set up for me, and a blank stack of paper waited. A badge holder handed me a pen and nodded toward the chair. The knowledge test wasn't recited aloud this time; it had to be written, word for word. The Sentinel's Creed. The poems. The history of the Tomb. The details of the Unknowns. The names of the generals and heroes buried in Arlington. All of it.

I sat in silence, pen scratching, my hand cramping as I wrote line after line. Every few minutes, a badge holder would step in, glance over my shoulder, then leave without a word. The silence was crushing. There was no encouragement, no hint of how I was doing. Only the weight of the words themselves, the memory drilled into me through months of repetition.

When I finally finished, I stood, papers in hand, and walked them over to the badge holders. They took them without a word and directed me back to the knowledge corner. The same place where I had stood hundreds of times before, reciting knowledge aloud as a "new guy." Now, I stood there again, this time waiting for them to decide if I had finally earned my place.

It wasn't perfection. It was never perfect. But I had given everything I had. And now, all that was left was the waiting.

When the outside performance and knowledge test were complete, I was still standing in the knowledge corner, heart pounding, waiting for something—anything. Instead of a verdict, one of the badge holders looked at me and said simply, "Go get changed. Get ready for your nightly duties."

It wasn't relief. It wasn't finality. It was just another order.

I hurried into the new man's room, pulling off the dress blues I had poured hours into and sliding back into my ACUs. My hands moved automatically, but my mind was still racing. Every button, every lace felt like a reminder of the mistakes I might have made that day. I could still hear the whisper of the micrometer gliding across my uniform, still see the faint nods and scribbles from badge holders as they circled me. I could still feel the weight of my rifle in my hands on the mat, each click of steel echoing louder in my chest than it had on the marble.

Once changed, I slipped back into the rhythm of nightly duties. Cleaning the quarters. Wiping down surfaces. Making sure everything was squared away for the next day. It was muscle memory by then, tasks I had done hundreds of times before. But that night, every sweep of the rag, every trip to empty a trash can, was blurred by the single thought that wouldn't leave me: Had I passed, or was I about to join the long line of names who didn't make it?

The minutes stretched into hours. My body was moving, but my head was somewhere else, replaying every step, every detail, over and over. I convinced myself I had failed. Then I convinced myself I hadn't. The pendulum swung back and forth until I felt sick with doubt.

Finally, close to 2300, the call came.

"Hull. Knowledge corner."

I dropped what I was doing and made my way there. My boots echoed faintly on the floor, louder to me than they had any right to be. The badge holders of my relief stood waiting, their faces set in the unreadable calm I had come to know so well. I snapped to position, eyes forward, waiting for the words that would decide everything.

And then—silence.

They let it hang there, stretching seconds into an eternity. My chest tightened. I could hear the blood rushing in my ears, louder than anything in the room. I braced myself for the worst, for the final blow that would send me back to Charlie Company, just another soldier who hadn't made it through.

Finally, the senior badge holder spoke.

"Congratulations, Hull. You passed."

For a second, I wasn't sure I'd heard him right. Relief crashed over me so hard I almost staggered. After twelve months of training, after endless nights of failure and correction, after thinking I would never master the patience and precision the Tomb demanded. I had passed.

And then, almost immediately, the solemn silence cracked. Smiles spread across their faces, and the senior badge holder barked out the words I had heard a hundred times before, but never like this:

"Three minutes, go."

This time it wasn't a drill. It wasn't practice. It was real.

I bolted for the new man room, the same way I had a hundred times before, only everything felt different. My hands didn't tremble with the fear of failing a stopwatch; they moved with the urgency of belonging. Blues on, tie cinched, scabbard clipped. Gloves in one hand, glasses in the other. By the time the badge holder bloused me in, I realized my lungs were burning. Not from the sprint, but from the surge of adrenaline.

When I stepped back into the knowledge corner, the air felt changed. For months, I had walked through those same halls as a "new guy," feeling the weight of scrutiny on my every move. But that night, for the first time, the atmosphere shifted.

The badge holders didn't stay stone-faced or reserved. As soon as the words "you passed" were spoken and I came back in my blues, the room broke into smiles and congratulations. Hands reached out to shake mine, claps landed on my shoulder, and for the first time in a year, I felt the divide between "new guy" and "badge holder" dissolve. Their voices weren't booming, but they were genuine. "Welcome to the line." "You earned it." "Proud of you." Each one carried weight, because these were men who had pushed me to the brink, who had refused to let me cut corners, who knew exactly what it had taken for me to get here.

Some of them teased me, too. Lighthearted, brotherly jabs that only came once you were finally part of the fold. I laughed for the first time in the quarters, not nervously, but because I finally belonged.

Even in that joy, the sense of the standard remained. There was no wild celebration, no breaking of the discipline that defined the Tomb. The next guard change still happened. The shoes still needed shining. Duties didn't vanish just because I had passed. But the atmosphere that night was different: it was the relief of a trial survived, the pride of a new Sentinel welcomed into the family, and the recognition that the badge now tied me forever to the Unknowns.

When I finally sat down late that night, exhaustion pulling me under, I let myself exhale fully for the first time in months. Twelve months of doubt, failure, corrections, and relentless pressure had brought me here. And now the badge would be on my chest.

That night, everything was different. For the first time, I wasn't just a candidate or a new guy shadowing others. I was a Sentinel. I had passed. The badge was mine. The Unknowns were in my charge, and I was guarding them for real. Standing there on the mat after hearing the words "Congratulations, Hull," I felt the weight settle in a new way. It was no longer the pressure of being tested. It was the responsibility of belonging to a lineage that stretched back generations.

And yet, as heavy as that moment was, life didn't stop to let me savor it. Only hours later, I was in a hospital room, stepping into a completely different role. The silence of Arlington, the marble, the steel, the centuries of tradition; suddenly, all of that gave way to fluorescent lights, rushing nurses, and the piercing cry of a newborn.

It was emotional whiplash in the purest form. One moment, I was etched into history by the badge on my chest. Next, I was holding my wife's hand as our first child entered the world. At the Tomb, silence was sacred; in that hospital room, the noise was sacred. Both carried weight. Both were unforgettable.

The badge had demanded sacrifice: long nights, patience, discipline, failure, and growth until finally, I met the standard. Fatherhood, I knew instantly, would demand all of that and more, but in ways no badge holder could prepare me for. At the Tomb, every step was measured. In that hospital, there was no drill, no script. It was messy and unpredictable, but it mattered just as much.

By the time I held my daughter, I understood something I couldn't have put into words before. In one day, two identities had been born. I was a Sentinel. I was a father. Both roles demanded vigilance, sacrifice, and devotion beyond myself. The Unknowns tied me to the past. My daughter tied me to the future.

Because of her birth, my badge ceremony was delayed. Most new Sentinels received theirs within days, sometimes even hours. For me, it would be months. I watched as others stood in front of their families, their fathers, their commanders, while the badge was pinned to their chest and their journey officially recognized. I had already earned it, but I hadn't been presented with it yet. The wait was harder than I expected.

When my time finally came, I was the only Sentinel being pinned that day. The last of the group I had started with. The room carried a weight all its own. My fellow "new guys" were there, now fellow badge holders. The chain of command stood in pressed uniforms, all the way up to the regimental commander and command sergeant major. Retired Sentinels filled in the ranks along the wall, watching with eyes that had once stood where I now stood.

And then my father stepped forward. His hands, worn from his own years of service, carried the badge that would mark me forever. When he pinned it to my chest, the metal felt heavier than anything I had ever worn. It wasn't just the weight of the badge. It was the weight of legacy—his, mine, and the Unknowns.

For a moment, the room was silent. Then came the applause, brief but powerful, echoing in the quarters. I glanced at my wife, holding our newborn daughter in her arms. The badge was mine, yes, but in that instant, it belonged to all of them. To my family, to the Sentinels who had trained me, to those who had tried and failed, and most of all to the Unknowns who rested in honored glory.

The badge ceremony marked the end of one journey, but the Creed reminded me daily that it was only the beginning. We recited it endlessly in training, word for word, until it was burned into memory. But it wasn't meant to stay on a page. The Creed was meant to be lived, line by line, on the plaza and beyond.

"My dedication to this sacred duty is total and wholehearted."

Those words demanded more than just showing up. Dedication wasn't partial, and it wasn't convenient. It meant sacrificing sleep to polish a shoe one more time. It meant pushing through exhaustion when your legs ached during a night shift. It meant putting the Tomb above your own comfort, above your own pride. I learned quickly that you couldn't fake wholehearted dedication—the badge holders saw through it instantly, and the Unknowns deserved nothing less.

"In the responsibility bestowed on me, never will I falter."

I faltered plenty in training. Botched uniforms, missed steps, and knowledge recitations that blurred together, but once I earned the badge, there was no room left for faltering. Not in the public eye. Not with the Unknowns depending on me. Every moment on the mat was a responsibility I couldn't hand back. The Tomb demanded consistency, even when fatigue, weather, or doubt tried to shake me.

"And with dignity and perseverance, my standard will remain perfection."

This line became my anchor. Perfection was the standard we all chased, knowing we would never fully reach it, but also knowing we could never stop trying. Perseverance meant enduring every failed inspection, every correction, every moment when I wanted to quit. Dignity meant carrying myself with respect through it all. Even in failure, even in silence.

"Through the years of diligence and praise and the discomfort of the elements, I will walk my tour in humble reverence to the best of my ability."

This line lived in my bones during the worst of the weather. The blizzard of 2009, the summers when the soles of our shoes threatened to melt, the rain that soaked through until blues clung heavy and cold. Through all of it, the Unknowns never left the plaza, so neither did we. Humble reverence was knowing that my discomfort was nothing compared to theirs.

"It is he who commands the respect I protect, his bravery that made us so proud."

Every salute, every step, every hour of silence was for them. Not for me, not for my badge, not for my peers. It was for the Unknowns. The men who had given everything, including their names. Their bravery was the reason I stood there, and the respect I carried wasn't mine to claim. It was theirs.

"Surrounded by well-meaning crowds by day…"

This line always struck me. Tourists with cameras, school groups chattering, families leaning on the rails. They came curious, sometimes reverent, sometimes not. Many never knew the depth of what they were seeing. They didn't see the long hours in the quarters, the blistered feet, the sweat behind the polish. But their presence reminded me that the Tomb belonged to the nation, not just to the Sentinels. Our silence taught when words never could.

"…alone in the thoughtful peace of night…"

This one, I lived deeply. At night, when the cemetery gates closed, the plaza changed. The crowd noise faded, and the silence settled like a weight. Under the amphitheater lights, I walked the shadow line with nothing but the Unknowns and the rhythm of my steels on stone. Those hours were different. Sacred in a way that no audience could touch. It was just me, the Unknowns, and the promise of eternal vigilance.

"…this soldier will in honored glory rest under my eternal vigilance."

The final line was never just poetry to me. Eternal vigilance meant that even when I left Arlington, the responsibility didn't end. The badge could be revoked if I failed to uphold the standard, even years later. That vigilance followed me into combat, into fatherhood, into being a therapist, into business. The Tomb had branded me with a standard that I carried for life.

Eternal vigilance wasn't just about guarding the Unknowns. It was about guarding the values they embodied.

We said the Creed every day. But once the badge was pinned, I realized I didn't just say it. I lived it. Each line carried a story, a memory, a burden, a lesson. And together, they became the framework of the Sentinel I had become, and the man I was still learning to be.

Chapter 5 – The Sacred Duty

Earning the badge was not an ending. It was a beginning. The very night I pinned it on, I realized the Tomb doesn't let you exhale for long. The moment the badge pressed into my chest, I was no longer training for the standard. I was carrying it.

The rhythm of life as a badge holder was measured in steels on marble. Each day began long before most visitors ever reached the cemetery gates. The first guard change of the morning came at 0800, but the plaza was alive well before then. The air at dawn carried a quiet anticipation. You could feel it in the way the light spilled over the white marble of the Amphitheater, in the way the shadow of the Tomb stretched long across the mat, in the way the stillness seemed to hold its breath. By the time the first Sentinel stepped onto the plaza, the stage was already set.

From the first heel click to the last, the mat demanded a rhythm as steady as the sunrise. Twenty-one steps down, twenty-one seconds paused, twenty-one steps back. It sounds simple, almost mechanical, when explained in words. But on the mat, it was anything but simple. Each twenty-one was its own vow, its own renewal of the promise that perfection was the standard, not the goal.

The steels in your shoes told the story. A clean, crisp strike on the marble rang sharp and true, echoing up into the colonnades of the Amphitheater. You could tell if a step was off just by the way the sound carried. A slightly duller click meant a heel hadn't been set perfectly. Too heavy a strike, and the sound broke the silence rather than blending into it. Even the public could sense the difference, though they might not know why. For us, that sound was everything. It was our metronome, our measure, the invisible hand keeping us in line with the generations of Sentinels who had walked before.

As the day wore on, the plaza shifted. Early in the morning, the cemetery was hushed, with only a handful of visitors leaning quietly against the chains. By midday, the hum of the crowd grew. Tour buses pulled in, and hundreds of voices buzzed against the silence of the plaza. Even then, the mat didn't change. The sequence remained the same: twenty-one, twenty-one, twenty-one. Yet every walk felt different depending on the crowd. Sometimes you could sense the awe as people fell silent at the first echo of steels. Other times, whispers persisted, cameras clicked, and children fidgeted behind the chains. None of it mattered. The mat was the constant.

Evening brought its own weight. As the crowds thinned and the shadows lengthened across the marble, the plaza grew quiet again. The last guard change, the evening BOLO, often carried a heaviness that felt different from the morning. It was the bookend to the day, the closing of a vigil that would begin again with the sunrise. Walking that last hour, you could almost feel the silence deepen, as if the Unknowns themselves were leaning closer in the stillness.

Walking the mat as a candidate had been an exercise in nerves. Every step was haunted by doubt—was I crisp enough, sharp enough, perfect enough? But once the badge was pinned to my chest, something shifted. The nervousness didn't vanish, but it transformed. I no longer felt like an intruder trying to measure up to the standard. I felt accepted by the mat. The marble no longer seemed to resist me; it seemed to recognize me. My steels no longer sounded tentative. They rang with the authority of someone who had been tested and found worthy.

That didn't mean the weight was gone. If anything, it was heavier. Now I wasn't just training for myself. I was representing the Unknowns, the Tomb, the Old Guard, the Army itself. But in that weight, there was a kind of peace. I belonged to the mat, and the mat belonged to me.

My first guard change as a badge holder came in the heat of summer, on a day when the air shimmered above the white marble like waves off asphalt. The plaza buzzed with hundreds of visitors pressed shoulder to shoulder behind the chains, their chatter rising and falling as they waited. For me, it was different from every walk before. This wasn't just another posting. This was my first change of the guard as a Sentinel, with the badge on my chest, representing not just myself but the brotherhood and the Unknowns.

The relief commander's voice broke the hum of the crowd, sharp and commanding. Every syllable carried across the plaza, crisp and practiced, demanding silence without asking for it. The moment the first words rang out, the crowd fell still.

I could feel sweat bead beneath my blouse, the wool clinging tight against my back. The sun was merciless, but I forced it from my mind. My focus was on the rifle, the weight of it familiar and steady in my hands, and the cadence of my steels striking the marble. Each click echoed off the plaza, cutting through the stillness. You can always tell from the sound if a step is precise or sloppy. The steel plates don't lie. That day, they rang true.

The sequence unfolded like muscle memory. Inspections were sharp and deliberate, every movement exact, the rifle spinning smoothly from my grip into the hands of the relief commander and back again without hesitation. The timing of heel clicks, the turns, the facings. All of it aligned perfectly, a rhythm born from the thousands of times I had drilled it.

But what struck me most wasn't the mechanics. It was the silence. The absence of any voice but the relief commander's, the absence of movement beyond the three of us on the mat. I was aware of the thousands watching, but in that moment, they might as well have been invisible. It was just us. The mat, the rifle, and the Unknowns.

When the final commands rang out and the change was complete, the plaza erupted again in hushed whispers and shifting feet, tourists already raising cameras to their faces. For me, it was something else entirely. Standing there in full blues, sweat stinging my eyes, chest heavy with pride, I knew I had crossed into a new chapter. I wasn't just walking anymore. I was a Sentinel in full, keeping the unbroken watch.

Life in the quarters was its own kind of crucible. The world above was marble, sun, and ceremony; below, in the cramped rooms beneath the Amphitheater, it was sweat, polish, steam, and steel. Evenings often blurred into each other. Rows of new guys and badge holders hunched over blouses, hats, and shoes, the hiss of steamers and the sharp scent of Kiwi polish mixing into the air. It was a rhythm of its own: the scrape of brushes, the click of micrometers against brass, the muffled laughter that broke through when someone cracked a joke about gigs or about how many hours of their life they'd spent staring at the same pair of shoes.

There was camaraderie in that grind. One guy might be working a stubborn scabbard while another leaned over to help measure a medal bar for the hundredth time. Shoe polish-stained fingertips like badges of effort, and it wasn't unusual to see someone nodding off at the bench, chin nearly in their blouse, only to be jolted awake by a badge holder reminding them that perfection doesn't sleep. In those moments, we weren't just individuals chasing a standard. We were a machine of discipline, all pushing toward the same finish line.

As a badge holder, the atmosphere shifted. I went from being the one scrutinized to the one doing the scrutinizing. The first time I leaned over a new guy's uniform, scanning for crooked seams or misaligned brass, I felt the weight of the responsibility settle on me. It wasn't about catching mistakes for the sake of it. It was about teaching the standard, carrying forward what had been drilled into me with relentless precision. Correcting a new guy wasn't easy. You could see in their eyes the same nerves I'd once carried. I knew that every adjustment, every tough critique, was an investment in whether they would succeed on the mat or vanish back to their company.

Badge holders weren't cruel in those corrections, but they were unrelenting. And now I understand why. The first time I told a new guy to fix his tie, or pointed out that his seam was off by a hair, I saw my old self reflected in him—tired, frustrated, but determined. That reflection reminded me that the standard wasn't mine to ease or change. It was mine to uphold.

Life in the quarters carried its own rhythm: uniforms being pressed, shoes being polished, quiet mentoring between badge holders and new guys. But as steady as that life was, the Tomb was never confined to the quarters or even to the daily walks on the mat. There were days when the watch expanded beyond the ordinary rhythm of guard changes and uniform workdays when the entire weight of the Army, the nation, and even the world seemed to converge on the plaza.

Those were the days of ceremonies.

Some of the heaviest moments on the mat weren't the ordinary guard changes. They were the high-profile ceremonies, the times when the eyes on you weren't just tourists with cameras but ambassadors, generals, and even the President of the United States.

I remember the French ambassador's wreath ceremony as vividly as if it happened yesterday. That morning, the plaza felt different—busier, heavier, charged. The ceremonial platoons from the other branches were already assembling, each one razor-sharp in their movements, every detail rehearsed down to the smallest flick of a wrist. They marched in from the front of the Tomb, their cadence echoing up the marble steps, filling the plaza with the steady rhythm of boots and the muted clatter of rifles carried in unison. The Army Band wasn't just sending a bugler that day. They had added a drummer for the cadence of taps. It was a scene that blended precision and gravity, a reminder that this wasn't just another guard change. It was a national moment.

For me, it meant hours of stillness. I stood in the green box, at ceremonial parade rest, my rifle angled in front of me, one hand covering the bayonet, the other pressing the weapon steady into position. The sun beat down, unrelenting, pressing heat into the wool of my uniform until it felt like armor. Sweat collected at the base of my neck, itching, but I didn't move. That was the standard. I had stood in storms before, but standing frozen under the crushing heat, with thousands of eyes and every camera lens focused forward, was its own kind of trial.

You pass the time differently in those moments. For me, it meant reciting knowledge silently in my head. The Creed, the poems, and the history of Arlington. Sometimes I focused on the pressure of my hand over the bayonet, counting breaths to keep the rifle rock-solid. Minutes blurred into hours until time itself felt like another test, daring me to falter. But I didn't. None of us did. And when the ambassador finally approached, laid the wreath, and the ceremony reached its crescendo with taps, I felt the pride of having endured the trial in silence.

Other ceremonies carried a different kind of weight. Veterans Day and Memorial Day were unlike anything else at Arlington. Those mornings, the air buzzed with anticipation before the first visitors even arrived. Security tightened. Helicopters hovered in the distance.

Secret Service agents lined the periphery. The President or Vice President would be arriving soon to lay the wreath. For us, the preparation wasn't about weapons or security. That wasn't our lane. Our job was precision, perfection, and silence in front of the nation's leaders.

Standing there, heels set into the marble, I felt the entire country watching through the eyes of those leaders. The Army Band played. The bugle called. And then the President stepped forward, laid the wreath, and saluted. It was a moment that connected the Unknowns to the highest office in the land, a reminder that no matter who occupied the White House, the Tomb remained the same—silent, steadfast, unbroken.

For Sentinels, those ceremonies weren't about politics or personalities. They were about the Unknowns. The presence of dignitaries only raised the stakes, forcing us to embody the highest standard of reverence. In those moments, the mat felt larger than life, stretching far beyond the chains of the plaza, binding the living and the fallen together before the eyes of the world.

But the story of the Tomb didn't end on the mat. Guarding in silence was only one part of the duty. The other was speaking. Carrying the message of the Unknowns beyond the marble, beyond the plaza, and into the lives of those who came to learn. For me, that meant stepping off the mat and into classrooms, auditoriums, and veterans' halls, where the lessons of sacrifice could be passed on.

Chapter 6 – Stories from the Tomb

One of the most rewarding parts of being a Tomb Guard wasn't standing the mat itself, but stepping off it to speak with the young people who came to Arlington on field trips. They arrived in packs. Sometimes, entire classes of wide-eyed fifth graders were shepherded by teachers, sometimes buses of middle or high school students still buzzing with the energy of the city tours they'd been on. Their voices carried across the plaza, curious and unfiltered in a way only children's voices can be.

The questions were often the same. *Do you really guard twenty-four hours a day? Do you guard in the rain? When was the Tomb built?* Each group seemed to carry the same list of curiosities, shaped by the research they had done in class before the trip or by the myths that swirl around the Tomb of the Unknown Soldier online. The answers, of course, never changed. Yes, the watch is twenty-four hours a day, seven days a week, through every kind of weather, and it has never stopped since 1926. But the way we delivered those answers mattered. We didn't just rattle them off mechanically. Each explanation was given with precision, and with the same weight and tone as if it were the very first time the question had ever been asked. Because for those kids, it *was* the first time. This was their introduction to the Tomb, to its legacy, and to the Sentinels who carried that legacy forward. We knew the impression we left could last a lifetime, and we wanted it to be one that inspired them.

Some questions revealed just how young and innocent they were. I'll never forget one girl who leaned over to her classmate, whispered loudly, and then finally asked me herself: *"Are you a robot?"* She couldn't reconcile how someone could stand so still, never flinch, never scratch, never move, even when the sun was blazing or the wind was cutting across the plaza. The whole group of girls giggled nervously at her bravery in asking, and I was given the opportunity to address them directly.

I crouched down a little so I was closer to their level and explained gently that no, we weren't robots. "We're very much human," I told them, "with emotions and feelings, just like you. But we train ourselves to keep them in check when we're on duty. We learn discipline, we learn focus, and we practice until standing still becomes second nature." Their eyes widened, the giggles fading into nods. I could tell the answer satisfied them, but more than that, it gave them a glimpse into the dedication that went into the role.

Sometimes their questions made me chuckle inwardly, even if my outward expression stayed controlled and professional. Kids wanted to know if we were allowed to scratch our noses while posted, or if we had to hold it in until the walk ended. They wanted to know if we could eat or drink during a shift, or if we could sneak in a bathroom break. To them, those were the pressing mysteries. Their laughter and innocence had a way of reminding me that while the Tomb was built on sacrifice, it also carried forward through education. Those questions showed that children were paying attention, curious about service and sacrifice in a way that mattered.

Teachers often hovered close during these exchanges, their eyes lighting up as they watched their students interact with us. Many of them later told me how meaningful it was for their kids to meet a real Sentinel and to hear, directly from us, what the Tomb represented. For the students, it transformed the Tomb from a marble monument into something alive. Something carried on the shoulders of soldiers standing right in front of them.

In those moments, I felt like more than a guard. I was a bridge. I wasn't just standing watch; I was handing down the story of the Unknowns to the next generation. That responsibility carried a weight of its own. These children would one day be voters, leaders, teachers, and parents themselves. If their first real impression of the Tomb was one of awe and respect, perhaps they would carry that forward and pass it along.

Sometimes, their laughter and lighthearted questions made me want to smile or laugh with them. Inside, I often did. But outwardly, I maintained the same calm, steady tone that the Tomb demanded. That contrast, the warmth of their curiosity, and the stoicism I had to maintain created a quiet balance. It reminded me that while we represented discipline and reverence, we were also human beings connecting with other human beings.

Looking back, those school tours were some of the most important parts of my time at the Tomb. The mat tested my discipline. The badge tested my endurance. But the children tested something different: my ability to inspire without fanfare, to teach without lecturing, and to show them that honor and sacrifice aren't abstract concepts, but living commitments. Every question, no matter how small, was a chance to plant a seed that might grow into understanding, respect, or even service someday.

And every time I answered, I carried the same truth with me: the Tomb wasn't just about us as Sentinels. It was about shaping the memory of the Unknowns for every generation to come. Even the ones still small enough to ask if we were robots.

If schoolchildren brought laughter and innocence to the plaza, veterans brought weight. Their presence shifted the air in ways no tourist crowd ever could. The questions of a fifth grader made you want to smile. The silence of an old soldier staring at the Tomb made you want to stand a little taller.

The contrast between civilians and veterans was stark, especially in the tone of their questions. Civilians wanted to know how long we could stand still, if we were allowed to scratch an itch, and if the changing of the guard happened while they slept. Veterans didn't care about myths. Their questions cut deeper. They asked about the grind of training, about the failures and the corrections, about what it demanded of your mind. They weren't interested in the ceremony as much as the crucible behind it.

One conversation still stays with me. Several active-duty Green Berets had come through. Their bearing was unmistakable: quiet confidence, strength without arrogance, the way they scanned everything without seeming to move their eyes. When they approached me after a guard change, the questions came quickly.

"So how long does it take to make it through?"

"What's the hardest part: mental or physical?"

"Do guys quit more because of the uniform stuff or because they just can't take the pressure?"

Their tone was nothing like civilians'. Civilians asked with curiosity; these men asked with recognition. They knew what it meant to live inside a standard that most of the world couldn't see. When I explained the balance of knowledge, uniform, and outside performance, they nodded like men who understood the hidden grind. One of them leaned a little closer and said, "Sounds a lot like our pipeline. Physical's the easy part. It's all mental."

That struck me. Here were some of the most elite soldiers in the world, comparing their own trials to what we endured at the Tomb. Their acknowledgment meant something. It reminded me that the weight of the badge wasn't just recognized by tourists. It carried respect among warriors who knew what it meant to suffer, to be broken down, and to rise again through discipline alone.

But not every veteran conversation was with men in their prime. Many of the most powerful encounters came with those who had long since put down the rifle.

The Honor Flights were among the most humbling. Buses rolled in, unloading groups of veterans from World War II, Korea, and Vietnam. They came in wheelchairs, some with oxygen tanks at their sides, others leaning heavily on canes. Their bodies were frail, but their eyes still carried the fire of soldiers. Many of them didn't ask questions at all. They simply thanked me for standing the watch, for carrying on the tradition, for remembering when so much of the country seemed to forget.

I watched men in their eighties and nineties try to rise from wheelchairs when the bugle sounded. Caretakers pressed their hands on their shoulders, urging them to stay seated, but more often than not, they waved the help away. They stood anyway. Trembling, leaning, sometimes clutching an oxygen tank in one hand while saluting with the other. Their salutes weren't sharp like they once had been, but they were heavy with meaning. The tears in their eyes said what words could not.

There was one Honor Flight in particular that has stayed with me. After a ceremony, a man approached slowly, his steps unsteady, his breathing labored. He didn't ask me about the Creed, the training, or the weather. Instead, he gripped my hand with surprising strength and told me his best friend's name. The name of a man who had never come home from Vietnam. He held on to my hand as though he were passing me something fragile and sacred.

"Every time you take a step out there," he said, his voice rough but steady, "you're carrying him too. Don't forget that."

I never did. That moment reminded me that the Unknowns represented not only those buried in Arlington without names, but also the unnamed in the hearts of veterans who still carried their losses decades later. The Tomb was not only their monument. It was their memory made visible in marble.

Many veterans thanked me even though I had never yet deployed. At first, I didn't know how to respond. How could I, who had not yet tasted combat, receive thanks from men who had left parts of themselves on foreign battlefields? But one veteran told me plainly: "You may not have deployed, but you're carrying the weight for those who didn't come back. That matters."

That statement reframed everything for me. It wasn't about comparing sacrifices. It was about carrying the memory forward, standing for those who could no longer stand for themselves.

Speaking with veterans was never casual. It was an exchange heavy with meaning. Each handshake, each salute, each word of gratitude reminded me that the Tomb connected generations. It tied my twenty-year-old self in dress blues to men who had stormed beaches, trudged through jungles, or frozen on mountainsides. It wasn't just the Unknowns I was guarding. It was every soldier whose name still lived in the hearts of those who had served beside them.

Despite the weight of the watch, there were moments of recognition that caught me completely off guard. Veterans carried silence, children carried curiosity, but sometimes the public or the Army itself tried to shine a light back on us. Those moments never felt like they belonged to me. They belonged to the Unknowns. Still, I can't deny that some of them made me smile in ways I hadn't expected.

The Virginia Travel Guide was one of those. I had no idea I'd even been photographed, let alone published. One afternoon, a package showed up at our place, addressed to me but with no clear sender. My wife at the time stood beside me, just as puzzled, as I slit the tape open. Inside was the familiar glossy smell of fresh print ink and paper clinging together. Like a brand-new book pulled off a shelf. Nestled inside was the Virginia Travel Guide of 2009.

I flipped it open casually, still unsure why it had been sent. Then I froze. There I was. Standing guard at the Tomb of the Unknown Soldier, captured mid-step in full dress blues. The image had been submitted by a photographer who had visited Arlington, and the editors thought enough of it to place me in the guide. With it came an extra photograph and a handwritten note of thanks from the staff who had worked on the publication.

I couldn't stop smiling. Not because it was me in the picture, but because it meant the story of the Unknowns had traveled into thousands of homes and hands across the state. People who had never set foot in Arlington might flip through that guide and stop at that page. Maybe they would pause long enough to read, to learn, to wonder. That was worth more than any personal recognition.

Around the same time, I was selected to be in the Army's Soldier of the Month Magazine. On the surface, it was a small recognition. Just one soldier among thousands across the Army who earned the honor in their respective months. But to me, it felt surreal. Tomb Guards lived in anonymity. Our creed demanded it. The badge was about devotion, not fame. Yet suddenly, I was standing for a photo shoot, answering interview questions for an article.

The magazine spread focused on the Tomb, not me personally, which was exactly how I wanted it. They inquired about our training process, failure rate, and the precision we strive for. I remember speaking alongside another badge holder as we tried to explain what it meant to endure the endless inspections, the "Three Minutes, Go" drills, and the sleepless nights memorizing knowledge. We were careful to frame every answer so that the spotlight always pointed back to the Unknowns. When they asked about what made the job hardest, I told them it wasn't the weather or the inspections—it was the weight of knowing that every step you took had to honor men who had given more than we ever could.

That became my default in those moments. Whenever someone tried to thank me personally for my service at the Tomb, I redirected it to the Unknowns. Not out of false humility, but because it was the truth. We earned the badge, yes, but the sacrifice we represented wasn't ours.

I remember one tour in particular that drove that point home. I had been asked to lead a group around the cemetery, explaining the history of the Tomb and the discipline required of Sentinels. It was a normal tour, families, friends, questions about the mat and the reliefs. Only at the end did someone quietly mention that one of the men in the group was a Medal of Honor recipient. I hadn't known. I had treated him just as I treated every other guest: with respect, but with the same focus on the Unknowns rather than on who was standing in front of me.

At the end of the tour, I snapped a salute to him and thanked him for his service. Before he could respond, his friend said proudly, "Do you know who this is? He's a Medal of Honor recipient."

I nodded, and with genuine respect, I repeated my thanks to him, but I also reminded them both that, at the end of the day, the Unknowns had sacrificed more than any soldier ever could. They gave not only their lives, but their very identities. The Medal of Honor recipient didn't argue or brush me off. He nodded firmly and agreed. Later, he even wrote me a letter of recommendation for my career, not because of anything special I had done for him, but because I had kept the focus where it belonged—on the Unknowns.

Those moments of recognition were humbling. They made me proud, but they also reminded me of the danger of pride. The badge was never about me. The Tomb was never about any of us. It was about sacrifice, about anonymity, about remembering those who had given everything and received no name in return. Recognition, when it came, was only meaningful when it served as another chance to redirect the nation's eyes back to the marble sarcophagus and the silence it guarded.

For me, the Virginia Travel Guide, the Soldier of the Month article, and even the handshake of a Medal of Honor recipient all meant the same thing: the Unknowns were being remembered. And that was the only recognition that ever mattered.

Recognition was always fleeting. A magazine spread, a travel guide photo, a handshake. They all passed quickly. But the real recognition, the kind that lasted, came from the weather itself. The elements didn't applaud. They tested you. They stripped away pretense and left only resolve. Standing the watch in perfect conditions was expected. Standing it when nature did everything in its power to break you. That was when the Unknowns were honored most.

The blizzard of 2009 was one of those tests. It didn't just snow; it consumed everything. For days, maybe close to a week, D.C. lay buried under ice and snow. The city shut down. Schools closed. Roads emptied. Even the cemetery gates are locked to the public. But the Tomb did not stop. It never had, and it never would.

Walking in that storm was brutal. The wind sliced across the plaza, turning every exposed patch of skin into fire. Snow whipped against my face, stinging like needles. Each step threatened to betray me. The mat was slick with a thin film of ice, steels ringing sharper than usual as they struck the frozen surface. Half the time, my only thought was simple: Don't slip. Don't fall. Keep moving.

When we weren't on the mat, we shoveled. Over and over again. Clearing snow from the chains, from the steps, from the mat itself, only for the storm to erase our work within minutes. Gloves are soaked through. Shoes froze stiff. My blues clung heavily against my body, the wool stiff with ice. Hours blurred together. Misery was constant. Yet in the heart of it, something strange happened: I found pride. I was miserable, cold, and exhausted, but I was walking. The Unknowns hadn't chosen comfort when they fell, and neither did we. Looking back, I'm glad I walked in that storm. It was one of the purest expressions of what it meant to be a Sentinel.

If winter was a test of endurance, summer was a trial by fire. July in Washington, D.C., is a furnace on its own. Add in a 100% wool uniform, starched and pressed within an inch of its life, and it became something else entirely. I remember one Tomb Guard who measured the temperature within their uniform using a meat thermometer. The inside of the uniform registered 145 degrees. One hundred and forty-five.

Heat radiated off the marble like an oven. Sweat poured down my back, stinging my eyes, pooling under my collar in places I didn't even know could sweat. Shoes softened against the mat, steels sticking slightly with each step. Breathing felt heavy, like pulling air through a furnace. Yet none of that mattered. The dedication to the Unknowns carried me forward, step after step.

There were days I thought the heat would break me. Days when the dizziness crept in and the sweat wouldn't stop, when the uniform clung like a second skin, and I wanted nothing more than relief. But quitting wasn't an option. The Unknowns hadn't chosen the weather of their sacrifice. We didn't choose ours either. Our duty was to walk, no matter the cost.

It was during those extremes —the snow that blinded, the heat that suffocated —that I understood the weight of the watch in a deeper way. Veterans, school kids, even former Tomb Guards often reminded me that what we were doing mattered. But in those moments of raw endurance, it wasn't words that carried me. It was the Unknowns themselves.

Back then, it was that thought, the sacrifice of others, that kept me moving. Now, years later, after combat tours and after losing brothers in Afghanistan, the weight of it all has caught up with me differently. I look back on those days in the storm or under the burning sun with a different kind of pride. I realize those walks weren't just about my endurance. They were about honoring every soldier who had endured worse. Who had given everything and never come home.

That was the quiet recognition. Not a magazine spread, not a photo, not an award. Just the knowledge that for one more hour, in ice or fire, the Unknowns had not been forgotten.

But the weather wasn't the only thing that left a mark. Brotherhood did too.

The bond of Sentinels doesn't end when you hang up the uniform. Years later, I've crossed paths with them in the most ordinary places. At the gym, in airports, at Society events. No matter where or when, the connection is instant. You notice the posture first, the way someone carries themselves. A handshake follows, firm and knowing. Few words are needed. It's not about swapping stories or proving anything. It's the unspoken: *You stood the watch. I stood it too.*

I remember visiting the quarters after I had long since moved on. Walking down those steps, the smell of polish and starch hit me like a wave, taking me back instantly. The new generation of Sentinels was there, heads bent over uniforms, binders in hand, shoes lined up by the dozens. They looked up when I walked in, eyes flickering with recognition. Not of me, but of what I represented: someone who had carried the burden before them. I laughed with them, shared small stories, and encouraged them to keep going. It reminded me of myself, hunched in those same rooms, convinced I would never measure up. Now I was the one telling them: *You can. Keep pushing. The badge is worth it.*

At Society events, I've seen older Sentinels. Men decades removed from the mat stand a little straighter when they meet someone who walked after them. The badge doesn't fade with time. It doesn't matter if you earned it in the 1960s or the 2000s; the bond is the same. That brotherhood bridged age, rank, even entire generations. In a world where so many connections fade with time, this one didn't.

That bond reassured me later in Afghanistan. Combat is chaos, stripped of ceremony, but the discipline of the Tomb stayed with me, and so did the knowledge that others before me had carried it into war. I wasn't the first Sentinel to trade the mat for the battlefield, and I knew I wouldn't be the last. In those moments when fear pressed hard, I thought of the Unknowns and of the brothers I'd trained beside. The ones who had made it and the ones who hadn't. Their presence steadied me, even half a world away from the marble of Arlington.

In civilian life, too, the brotherhood lingered. There were days when doubt crept in, when the weight of fatherhood, work, or life after service felt overwhelming. Then I'd run into another Sentinel, and in that brief handshake, in that shared smile, I was reminded: the standard I carried wasn't mine alone. Others still bore it. Others still upheld it. And together, we formed a chain that stretched back to 1926 and forward to every new generation who would step onto the mat.

The storms pass. The heat fades. The uniform gets put away. But the brotherhood that endures.

Chapter 7 – The Bond of Sentinels

Even after leaving Arlington, the brotherhood of Sentinels never disappeared. The bond was too strong, too enduring to fade just because time or distance carried us away from the mat. Some of us found it through visits back to the quarters, while others discovered it through quiet conversations when we happened to cross paths at events or in uniform. In recent years, that connection has taken shape in a tradition we call "Cocktail Hour."

It isn't formal, not like the reunions hosted by the Society every two years. Instead, it's a Zoom call of Sentinels from across the decades, some still young and sharp in their twenties, others older with gray hair, canes at their side, and grandchildren wandering in and out of the background. Everyone logs in from different places. Living rooms, kitchens, cluttered garages, and even the occasional backyard porch. Some raise a beer, others sip water or coffee. A few just sit quietly, content to listen. The screen fills with familiar faces and unfamiliar ones alike, but the badge on each of us ties the generations together instantly.

The conversations jump across time. A man with a low badge number, earned in the 1970s, recounts walking the mat in the middle of a snowstorm, shoveling until his hands went numb. Without missing a beat, a younger Sentinel chimes in, comparing it to the blizzard of 2009. The names of the storms are different, the decades apart, but the hardships are the same. Everyone nods, smiling, because we all know what it means to walk twenty-one steps through driving snow with the Unknowns as your only witness.

Sometimes the younger guys will joke about how much harder inspections were in their era, and the older ones laugh, shaking their heads. "It was the same," one of them always says. "The standard hasn't changed. It just feels harder when you're the one being tested." And he's right. Whether you carried Badge Number 200 or Badge Number 600, the weight of perfection pressed just as heavily.

What strikes me most during these Cocktail Hours isn't the stories themselves, but the humility behind them. No one brags. No one tries to elevate their own service. Every story circles back to the same truth: it was never about us. It was about the Unknowns. We may have carried the badge in different eras, but we all carried the same standard, and we all left pieces of ourselves on that mat.

Some of the older Sentinels who join these calls can no longer travel. Age, illness, and the years have taken their toll. For them, this Zoom screen is the only way to sit with their brothers and sisters again. More than once, I've sat there listening to a man decades my senior, his voice cracking with age, telling a story about his time on the mat. You could see the emotion in his eyes—this was his way of coming home. That touched me deeply. It reminded me that one day, I too will be older, maybe unable to make the trip to Arlington, but still tied to the badge and the men and women who wear it.

There's something powerful in knowing that this bond doesn't just live in the prime of our youth. It carries us all the way into old age, when memories fade and bodies fail, but the Creed still echoes. These calls prove the badge endures far longer than a career. It outlasts deployments, marriages, children, and even health.

I remember one call in particular where an older Sentinel shared that he hadn't spoken about the Tomb in years. His health kept him from traveling to reunions, and most people in his daily life didn't understand what it meant to be a Sentinel. But on that screen, surrounded by others who knew the silence of the mat and the sting of inspections, he found his voice again. For him, those two hours weren't just a conversation—they were a return to a family he thought he'd lost. Watching him speak, I felt both humbled and honored to be part of that moment.

For me, those hours are more than catching up. They're reminders of responsibility. When I see men in their seventies or eighties, their voices shaky but their pride unbroken, I realize I am carrying their legacy forward just as much as my own. They walked before me. I carry the watch after them. And one day, some younger Sentinel will sit across a screen from me, listening as I tell stories about the blizzard of 2009 or my first nervous walk on the mat. The cycle continues, unbroken, because the bond is unbroken.

Even though I haven't yet been to one of the official reunions, I know what I'll find when I do. The faces may be older, the uniforms replaced by civilian clothes, but the bond will feel the same as it does on those calls. Timeless. Immediate. A connection that doesn't fade with the years, just like the Creed itself.

For Sentinels, brotherhood isn't just nostalgia. It's a living tether that runs through every badge number, every generation. And when we gather, whether online, in person, or simply by chance meeting, we're reminded that the mat doesn't just belong to one class or one time. It belongs to all of us, forever tied to the Unknowns.

And perhaps that's what makes it most humbling. You can earn your badge at twenty years old, still strong and full of fire, but decades later, that badge will still rest heavily on your chest, binding you to men and women who carried the same weight long before and long after you. That's what Cocktail Hour reminds me of every time: the watch may end for each of us individually, but the brotherhood, the eternal vigilance, never does.

Even after those Cocktail Hours ended, I always carried the same thought with me: this bond needed a foundation strong enough to outlast time, distance, and circumstance. Those virtual gatherings weren't random. They were created by Gavin McIlvenna, one of the four founders of the Society of the Honor Guard, Tomb of the Unknown Soldier. He recognized that many Sentinels, especially older ones dealing with physical ailments or limited mobility, could no longer travel to Arlington or reunions in person. The Cocktail Hours gave them a way to reconnect, to swap stories, and to relive the bond that had shaped them decades earlier. Hearing their voices across a screen, some frail with age but still strong with conviction, reminded me that being a Sentinel never truly ended.

That spirit of keeping the bond alive was exactly what led Gavin and three others, COL Neale Cosby, Richard Azzaro, and Meredith Smith, to establish the Society of the Honor Guard, Tomb of the Unknown Soldier (SHGTUS) on March 29, 1999. Their mission was simple but profound: to create a living organization where former Tomb Guards could continue serving by educating the public about the Tomb and supporting Sentinels who stood the eternal watch. They knew the bond forged at Arlington was too rare and too sacred to leave scattered. It needed a home.

The Society became that home.

Their founding vision has shaped everything the Society does today. Whether it's publishing historical resources, giving talks in schools, providing support to current Tomb Guards, or honoring the families of those who have passed, SHGTUS ensures that the standard of "eternal vigilance" lives on beyond the mat. I've seen it firsthand. When a Sentinel passed, the Society immediately stepped in to comfort his family, handle details, and make sure he was honored properly. It wasn't loud, it wasn't flashy, but it was dignified. Just like the watch itself.

The Society also connects us across generations. Newsletters share stories, memorial notices, and reflections from both active Sentinels and retirees. Forums and events allow us to ask questions, relive memories, and pass advice down the line. For older Sentinels, it is sometimes the only way they can still feel the rhythm of the mat in their lives. For younger ones, it's a way to realize they are part of something bigger than their own badge number.

Their public outreach is equally important. Members frequently speak in classrooms and civic halls, telling the story of the Unknowns and what it meant to guard them. They ensure that generations of Americans who may never set foot in Arlington still carry a piece of its silence with them. And each year, the Society organizes memorial events, both at Arlington and across the nation, where former Sentinels lay wreaths, share words, and continue the tradition of remembrance.

What strikes me most is how the Society mirrors the very essence of the watch. Just as the Tomb is guarded day and night without fail, the Society ensures the memory and responsibility of Sentinels never ends. The mat may no longer be under our feet, but the standard still is. In many ways, the Society is the unseen relief. Always present, always ready, and carrying forward the mission when individual Sentinels move on.

For me, the Cocktail Hours, the newsletters, and the ceremonies are reminders that once you've carried the badge, you never stand alone again. The Society keeps us connected—not just to one another, but to the Unknowns we all swore to protect.

The bond of the badge didn't end when I left Arlington. It followed me into the wider Army, cropping up in the most unexpected places. Out of the millions of soldiers in uniform, only a few hundred of us carried the Tomb Guard Identification Badge. Yet somehow, no matter where I went, it felt like we always managed to find each other.

My fondest memory came during my second deployment to Afghanistan with the 101st Airborne Division. We were on a forward operating base (FOB)—dust, plywood, and Hesco barriers, the kind of place that felt more temporary than permanent. One morning, during PT, I was stretching off to the side when I heard a voice cut through the shuffle of boots and the thud of running feet.

"Brace!"

The word hit me like a lightning bolt. For anyone else on that base, it was meaningless. But for a Sentinel, it was an order you didn't ignore. Without thinking, I snapped to the position of attention, dropped what I was holding, and froze. My heart hammered, not because of the command itself, but because of what it meant: there was another badge holder here.

I turned my head just enough to catch sight of him— Chase Neely, Badge #553. He was grinning as he slowed his jog, the desert sun bouncing off his PTs. The tradition of "brace" had started long before my time, but it lived on in every generation. Originally, it was a practical command, used in the quarters to stop a Sentinel from heading out the door if something was wrong with his uniform. A gigged ribbon, a loose thread, a crooked tie— "brace" froze him in place until the problem was fixed. Once corrected, the badge holder would give the command "unbrace," and the guard would continue on his way.

Over the years, it had become something more. A ritual of respect, a little game of humility and honor. A lower-numbered badge holder, meaning someone who had earned the badge before you, had the right to brace you anytime, anywhere. You stopped immediately, no excuses, no questions asked. You didn't move until they released you. It was a reminder that no matter how far you'd gone in the Army, no matter your rank or position, the badge number carried its own weight.

Neely let me stand there just long enough for the humor to land before laughing and saying, "Unbrace." I relaxed, and in that moment, we were no longer just two soldiers on deployment. We were Sentinels again, back in the quarters, bonded by a tradition only a handful of men and women in the world truly understood.

We connected a few more times during that deployment, grabbing chow together when we could, swapping stories about our time at the Tomb. The conversations never lingered on small talk. With Sentinels, you didn't have to waste time proving yourself. You already knew what the other had endured: the long nights in the knowledge corner, the pain of uniform gigs, the silence of the mat. Instead, we talked about the details—who our relief commanders were, how many months training had taken us, the quirks of the badge holders who had broken us down and built us back up.

When we redeployed, Neely and I met up again back stateside. Seeing another badge holder in garrison after surviving the chaos of Afghanistan reinforced what I already knew: the Tomb bond wasn't just ceremonial. It was real, and it traveled with you no matter how far you went from Arlington.

That bond transcended rank in a way nothing else in the Army did. Over the years, I met badge holders who had risen to the highest levels. Commanders, sergeants major, and even colonels. When we discovered one another, the formalities of rank didn't vanish, but something deeper settled in. The conversations were different. A colonel with a badge on his chest treated me, an E-4 at the time, with the kind of respect that came from knowing we had both walked the same marble. They shared insights into leadership, stories from their careers, and advice on how to grow into the kind of leader the Army needed.

That guidance was never about arrogance or pulling rank; it was about stewardship. They saw in me what they once had been: a young Sentinel, still carrying the lessons of the mat into the wider Army. Their willingness to treat me as an equal, to take time to teach me, was one of the greatest gifts the Tomb ever gave me outside of Arlington.

Finding Sentinels in the wider Army was like finding family in a crowded room. You didn't have to ask questions. You didn't have to explain yourself. One look, one handshake, one word— "brace"—and you knew. The badge number on your chest might have been different, but the standard was the same. Always.

The Tomb Guard Identification Badge is unlike any other in the Army. It is one of the rarest awards, and unlike most decorations, it can be revoked. Even years after a Sentinel has left Arlington. That knowledge stays with you for life. The standard doesn't end when you take off the uniform or when your last walk is finished. It follows you into every role, every responsibility. The badge isn't a souvenir. It is a covenant, a daily reminder that perfection is the standard and that vigilance must endure.

That truth shaped my habits long after I left the plaza. Every morning, I still pause when I lace my shoes. I take a breath and remind myself of the mat. The rhythm of twenty-one steps, the silence of the Unknowns, the promise never to falter. It's my way of putting the "badge on" again, even when no one else is watching. That ritual keeps me anchored. It reminds me that the standard belongs not to the past, but to the present moment I'm living in.

The lessons carried into every chapter of my life. In Afghanistan, precision and discipline became survival. The details I had once obsessed over in uniforms and rifles translated into double-checking weapons, radios, and movements under fire. The refusal to cut corners, the persistence to endure long hours of discomfort. These saved lives in combat just as surely as they once upheld the watch in Arlington.

Later, when I became a therapist, the badge reminded me of the weight of silence. Just as I once stood in stillness on the mat, I learned to sit in silence with someone else's pain, honoring it without rushing to fill the space. The patience forged in Arlington became the patience that allowed me to walk with others through their darkest moments.

And in fatherhood, the badge became a different kind of compass. Every time I looked at my children, I felt the standard pressing on me again. Not in the shine of a shoe or the angle of a rifle, but in the responsibility to never falter in their eyes. The Tomb taught me devotion beyond self, and that devotion became the heart of how I tried to parent.

The badge shaped me because it was never about me. It was about the Unknowns. About living in a way that honored their sacrifice. That is the weight I carried then and still carry now.

Looking back, I know the badge was never the end of a journey. It was the beginning of a lifelong duty.

I still catch myself in front of the mirror, adjusting a tie knot until it sits flush, tugging a seam until it's just right, or checking the shine of a shoe no one will ever grade. I don't do it because someone is watching. I do it because the Tomb is still with me. The standard remains.

Sometimes, in the quiet of a morning, I hear the echo of steels in my mind. The sharp click of heel to marble, the sound that once defined my every step. And in that sound, I remember: I am still a Sentinel. I am still guarding the Unknowns. Not on the mat, not in dress blues, but in the way I live, the way I serve, the way I carry their memory forward.

The badge is not a decoration to be set aside. It is a covenant. It is a lifelong weight, a lifelong honor, and a lifelong duty. And though my watch on the mat has ended, my eternal vigilance has not.

Chapter 8 – Mental Toughness

Arriving at the 101st Airborne Division after my time in the Old Guard was like stepping into another world. At the Tomb, every movement was calculated, every crease intentional, every silence sacred. In the 101st, the tempo was different—faster, looser, rough around the edges in a way that line units were meant to be. Soldiers spoke louder, laughed harder, and cut corners without thinking twice. To them, garrison life was just filler between the real work of training and deploying.

For me, the adjustment was jarring. I still carried myself like a Sentinel. Posture straight, uniform, tight, boots polished so well you could see your reflection. Old habits followed me, whether I wanted them to or not. In formation, I'd catch myself glancing down the line, correcting posture in my head the same way I used to watch new guys at the Tomb. More than once, I caught myself bracing uniforms instinctively, my hands twitching to square away a crooked pocket flap or twisted bootlace.

At first, the guys in my squad thought it was funny. "Hull, you're wound too tight," they'd say, or, "Relax, this isn't D.C." Some even teased me, calling me "pretty boy" for polishing my boots past what anyone thought was necessary. But I couldn't turn it off. The Tomb had burned the standard into me too deeply. I wasn't polishing for show. I was polishing because that's what I did. What I owed the men who trained me and the Unknowns I had once guarded.

Then came inspection week. Our Platoon Sergeant and Platoon Leader were making their rounds, the kind of check most soldiers dreaded. Guys scrambled the night before, spit-shining boots half-heartedly and pressing uniforms just enough to get by. I took a different approach. I spent hours on my boots until they looked like liquid glass. I pressed my uniform until it could have cut paper. When the morning came, I stood ready. My gear squared away, my appearance spotless, my posture set like I was back in Arlington.

When the inspection team reached me, I noticed the grin spread across my Platoon Sergeant's face before he said a word. My boots caught the light and reflected it like a mirror. Every detail of my uniform was razor-sharp. Then, just for myself, I reached into my pocket and pulled out a micrometer. The same kind we used at the Tomb, and started measuring my ribbon bar while they inspected me.

My Team Leader nearly doubled over laughing. "Hull, you're insane," he said under his breath. But my Platoon Sergeant just shook his head with a smile. He understood. He wanted that kind of standard in his formation.

That inspection changed things for me. A week later, I was promoted to replace my Team Leader. Not because I was the fastest runner or the loudest voice, but because I could function in combat and in garrison, and I carried my standards with me everywhere I went. My Platoon Sergeant valued that. He expected us to fight hard when deployed, but he also wanted a platoon that looked sharp, disciplined, and professional in garrison. I showed him both were possible.

The Tomb had taught me that perfection was the only acceptable goal, even when no one else was looking. In the 101st, that discipline translated into respect. Soldiers who once teased me for being "too strict" started coming to me for help with their uniforms. They realized that the extra attention to detail wasn't just about looking good. It was about taking pride in yourself, your unit, and the men you fought beside. And when it came time to deploy, that same relentless attention to detail carried over into the field. It was never just about spit and polish. It was about survival, leadership, and earning trust.

The 101st was a far cry from the marble plaza of Arlington, but in many ways, it was the perfect testing ground for what the Tomb had forged in me. Standards weren't meant to stay locked away at the Unknowns' side. They were meant to be carried forward. To combat, to leadership, to every part of Army life.

Stepping into college classrooms after the Army felt like walking into another world. Gone were the uniforms, the cadence, the strict chain of command. In their place were backpacks slung over one shoulder, coffee cups balanced on notebooks, and classmates who treated deadlines as flexible suggestions. For me, though, the habits forged on the mat didn't vanish when I traded dress blues for jeans and a sweatshirt. The Tomb had carved a rhythm into me. Attention to detail, structure, and precision. That became my anchor even in an environment that thrived on improvisation.

Most mornings started the same. I'd arrive early, binder in hand, every tab labeled, every assignment neatly tucked into its place. While others slid in late, fumbling for pens or flipping through crumpled notes, I already had my materials laid out in order, like uniforms prepared for inspection. It wasn't about showing off. It was simply how I functioned. To me, preparation was respect: for the professor, for the class, and for myself.

That difference stood out most during group projects. Group work in college was chaos disguised as collaboration. Some students thrived on last-minute brainstorming, others disappeared until the night before the deadline, and a few tried to coast without lifting a finger. For me, there was no coasting. I approached every project like a mat walk: deliberate, step-by-step, no room for shortcuts.

One project in particular still sticks with me. It was a psychology course that required a case study presentation. Our group of five met in the library to plan, but after ten minutes, the conversation drifted into weekend plans and half-hearted jokes. Papers were scattered across the table, laptops opened more to social media than research. I felt my frustration rise. Not because they weren't smart, but because they weren't focused. To me, every wasted minute was like a sloppy heel click on the mat, a visible flaw in the standard.

So I did what I knew how to do: I built a structure. I divided the project into sections, assigned roles, and set deadlines. I created a checklist that mapped every step from research to presentation slides. It was, in essence, a drill sequence. Each person is responsible for a precise movement, each deadline a cadence mark in the process. Some rolled their eyes, muttering that I was "too intense" or "acting like we were in the Army." But others, the ones who had been panicking quietly about the assignment, seemed relieved. They finally had a plan they could follow.

In the end, the presentation went smoothly, not because everyone suddenly became disciplined, but because the structure carried them. Afterward, the professor pulled me aside and complimented the organization, noting how rare it was to see a group presentation executed with such clarity. My classmates didn't say much, but I could see the difference: even those who thought my approach was overkill admitted it made their lives easier.

That pattern repeated itself often. My precision frustrated some but impressed others. Professors appreciated it. They saw in my papers and projects the kind of consistency that made grading easy. Citations were exact, formatting flawless, arguments laid out like steps in a drill sequence. I wasn't the smartest student in the room, but I was often the most prepared, and that preparation paid off.

Among peers, reactions varied. Some joked that I was "the guy who overdid it," showing up with color-coded notes and drafts finished a week early. But there were also moments when the same classmates who teased me would call the night before a deadline, asking for help because they knew I had already done the work. I never turned them away. Just like in the quarters at the Tomb, where older badge holders guided new guys, I felt a responsibility to help those who hadn't yet learned the value of discipline.

Even outside of projects, the Tomb's influence was obvious in my daily routine. While others crammed at the last minute for exams, I reviewed steadily, the way I had once repeated the Sentinel's Creed until it was etched into memory. While others pulled all-nighters fueled by energy drinks, I worked methodically, starting early so I wouldn't need to panic. That method wasn't glamorous, but it gave me a calmness others envied when test day came.

There were times, of course, when I wondered if I was out of place—if maybe I should relax, go with the flow, let things slide. But then I'd remember the mat. At Arlington, there was no "good enough." There was no room for almost-right. That standard had become part of me, and I wasn't about to abandon it just because others didn't share it.

College wasn't combat. It wasn't the Tomb. But in its own way, it tested the same qualities: persistence, patience, and the ability to hold yourself to a standard when no one else demanded it. I learned that perfection might never be fully reached in academia any more than it had been on the plaza, but the pursuit of it—step by step, page by page—made all the difference.

Looking back, I realize those classrooms were another proving ground. Just as the mat had taught me discipline in silence, college taught me discipline in dialogue. How to balance structure with flexibility, how to lead without ordering, how to carry the Sentinel's standard into a world that didn't even know it existed. In the end, it wasn't just about grades or projects. It was about showing myself that the lessons of the Tomb could survive anywhere. Even in a classroom full of unpolished shoes and crumpled notes.

Starting my PhD program felt less like walking into a classroom and more like stepping back into the Tomb. The expectations were high, the standards relentless, and the margin for error razor-thin. Each assignment felt like a uniform inspection. You could hand in something sloppy, but it would be ripped apart, and you'd pay the price.

The long nights became familiar again. I'd sit in front of my computer, the glow of the screen burning my eyes, a cold cup of coffee sitting untouched beside me. Deadlines pressed in, my fingers hovered over the keyboard, and every keystroke felt like a step on the mat. Measured, deliberate, without room for shortcuts.

There were moments when the work was kicked back to me, marked with comments that felt like a gig sheet covered in red ink. Whole sections of writing needed revision, entire arguments had to be reshaped, and some days it seemed like no amount of effort would ever be enough. It reminded me of standing in the knowledge corner, stumbling through a recitation, the badge holder's silence weighing more than any shouted correction. But just like at the Tomb, I didn't quit.

Still, I'd be lying if I said I carried the weight alone. The truth is, I had someone at my side through all of this: my fiancée. There were nights when frustration hit so hard, I wanted to slam the laptop shut and walk away. The doubt whispered that maybe I didn't belong here, that maybe I had taken on more than I could carry. And every time, her voice cut through that noise. She reminded me why I started, why finishing mattered, and why I was capable of doing the work.

Her encouragement was never dramatic. It was steady, almost like the quiet nod of a badge holder after a correction—subtle, but enough to keep me moving. Sometimes she sat beside me in silence, just keeping me grounded as I typed. Other times, she reminded me to breathe, to step back, to take the work one piece at a time instead of being crushed by the whole. Just as I once needed another Sentinel to blouse my top in order to buckle my belt before stepping onto the mat. I needed her words to keep me walking this academic path.

Each chapter I drafted felt like a test at the Tomb: the uniform, the knowledge, the outside performance all rolled into research, analysis, and writing. The feedback from professors was just as sharp as the critiques from badge holders. But the lessons I had carried from Arlington—discipline, persistence, humility—gave me the endurance to keep going. And the support from her gave me the balance to not lose myself in the process.

I haven't reached the dissertation defense yet, but I know I will. The same way I once knew, standing on the marble in the dead of night, that quitting was not an option. The mat taught me that perfection may never be fully reached, but the standard must always be pursued. The PhD has taught me that even the pursuit itself is worthy, especially when you're not walking it alone.

Chapter 9 – Honor and Sacrifice

That pursuit of perfection was more than discipline—it was an expression of honor. The Tomb demanded not only toughness but also a life lived in devotion, shaped by both faith and service.

For me, honor wasn't something I discovered at Arlington; it had been shaping me long before I ever laced steels or carried a rifle. My understanding of honor came from two worlds that seemed separate at the time but were deeply connected in practice: my family's military legacy and my quiet faith in Pagan values.

My grandfather had fought in Korea and Vietnam. My father had served in Mogadishu and Cuba. Neither of them ever sat me down to lecture me about "honor," but I learned by watching how they carried themselves. My grandfather rarely spoke of combat, but when he did, he spoke not of medals or glory but of the men he fought beside. My father was the same, focused less on his own experiences and more on the weight of duty. Their silence wasn't avoidance. It was reverence. From them, I learned that honor was less about what you said and more about how you lived.

At the same time, my Pagan worldview was quietly shaping how I interpreted those lessons. I didn't call it "Norse Paganism" back then. It was simply Pagan, rooted in the idea that a person's worth was measured by their honor. A man's reputation lived longer than his body. The sagas and stories whispered the same truth I saw in my father and grandfather: keep your word, fulfill your duty, and live with courage, because that was the only legacy that endured. The gods and ancestors judged not by what you claimed, but by how you carried yourself when no one was watching.

Those two streams of influence—family and faith—merged fully when I arrived at the Tomb. Arlington allowed no shortcuts. A single loose thread, a single misaligned medal, a single word missed in a recitation could mean the difference between staying in training or being sent back. There was one moment in particular, early in my training, when a badge holder stopped me during inspection. My tie sat just a hair off-center. He didn't yell. He didn't berate me. He simply looked at me and said, "Fix it." I wanted to argue, to explain that it was barely noticeable, but instead I adjusted it in silence. That was the moment it hit me: honor wasn't about what I thought was "good enough." It was about living up to a standard higher than my own comfort. From that point forward, I stopped trying to defend my mistakes. I owned them and worked to correct them.

The Army's definition of honor was written in the values every soldier memorized: loyalty, duty, respect, selfless service, honor, integrity, and personal courage. My Pagan definition was less formal but no less binding: keep your word, fulfill your oaths, live with courage, and leave behind a name worth remembering. Though they came from different traditions, both pointed to the same truth—honor is not recognition. It is a responsibility.

At the Tomb, that truth was reinforced daily. The badge, the uniform, the precision—none of it was about me. It was about the men who gave all, even their identities. Our purpose was not to be seen but to ensure the Unknowns would never be forgotten.

That reality transcended faith as well. I never once heard a Sentinel talk about his personal religion while on duty. Men of many beliefs walked the mat. Christian, Jewish, Pagan, or no faith at all, and yet none of that mattered. We were all bound to the same duty. Chaplains came through the cemetery often, especially during wreath ceremonies, and their prayers were welcomed, but their words were always directed at the Unknowns, not at us. That distinction mattered. Our personal spirituality remained private because the mission itself was sacred. The Unknowns didn't belong to one creed or denomination. They belonged to the nation. And in guarding them, our faith was expressed not through words but through the silence of service.

Honor wasn't something you wore; it was something you lived. It wasn't a medal, a badge, or a title. It was the way you carried yourself when no one else was looking, the way you endured without complaint, the way you sacrificed without expecting thanks. That, to me, was honor.

But no matter how much the Tomb demanded of us. No matter the long hours, missed holidays, or aching shoulders from a rifle carried motionless in the rain, our sacrifices were nothing compared to the Unknowns'. Every day, as I looked down at the marble, I reminded myself: they had given everything. Their sacrifice was ultimate. Ours was simply to honor it.

The Unknowns carried a weight that could never be measured. Each crypt told a story not only of war, but of absence. Beneath the sarcophagus lay the Unknown from World War I. He was buried on November 11, 1921, carried in a solemn procession from France to Arlington. His identity lost to history; his sacrifice became a stand-in for every soldier who vanished into the mud of Flanders or the shattered trenches of the Western Front. When I walked the mat, I often thought of his mother—wherever she had lived, whatever her name was—never knowing which battlefield her son fell on, never receiving certainty of his fate. That was the true cost of his sacrifice: not only his life, but the silence left behind in every family that never had answers.

Behind the sarcophagus, three more crypts remind us of what was lost in later wars. The World War II Unknown was buried in 1958. His crypt represents the thousands who were lost across Europe and the Pacific. Men swallowed by oceans, destroyed in bombings, left unclaimed on battlefields stretching from Normandy to Okinawa. Standing guard, I sometimes thought of the children who grew up without fathers after those campaigns. Their absence stretched into decades. For them, the Unknown was not just a soldier. They were every soldier.

The Korean War Unknown, buried the same day in 1958, embodied another generation's grief. Korea was often called the "Forgotten War," yet for the families of the missing, nothing was forgotten. The Unknown buried at Arlington represented thousands of soldiers who vanished on frozen ridges, in prisoner of war camps, or in battles where recovery was impossible. Guarding his crypt reminded me that sacrifice does not diminish with time. Even if a war fades from public memory, the weight of loss never does for the families who bear it.

Then there was the Vietnam Unknown. Interred in 1984 but exhumed in 1998 when advances in DNA testing confirmed his identity as Air Force 1st Lt. Michael Blassie. His return to his family was a moment of justice long delayed, but it also left a powerful emptiness at the Tomb. His crypt now bears the inscription: *"Honoring and keeping faith with America's missing servicemen, 1958–1975."* Standing above that empty crypt reminded me that sacrifice doesn't always end in finality. Sometimes it endures in uncertainty, in the endless waiting of families who still don't know where their sons or daughters rest.

Together, these crypts are not just stone. They are absence is made permanent. The Unknowns gave their lives without recognition, without names etched in granite. They were stripped of even the most basic dignity of identity, yet their sacrifice became the nation's sacred symbol. When I stood guard, rifle in hand, it wasn't only about the past. It was about the silence of mothers who never received word, of wives who stared at doors that never opened again, of children who grew old carrying questions that would never be answered.

That silence lived in the plaza. It pressed against your chest every time you walked the mat. The shuffle of tourists behind the chains fell quiet because even they felt it, though they couldn't explain it. For us as Sentinels, the silence was not emptiness—it was weight. It was the unspoken burden of families who never saw closure, and of soldiers who had given more than anyone could repay.

Every step. Twenty-one forward, twenty-one seconds, twenty-one back. It was a reminder that our small sacrifices were only shadows of theirs. They bore the true cost. We bore the vigil.

But sacrifice wasn't just an idea carved into stone; it was lived out in the rhythm of the watch. At the Tomb, sacrifice meant standing in every kind of weather, pushing through fatigue, and polishing a uniform until dawn, knowing you'd only wear it for a single walk. It also meant missing holidays—days that the rest of the country spent gathered around tables, exchanging gifts, or sleeping in late.

I remember one Christmas in particular. The quarters were filled not with decorations but with the faint scent of starch and shoe polish. No tree and no presents. just the rhythmic scrape of brushes on leather and the hiss of irons pressing creases. Outside, the plaza was silent, the marble catching the pale winter light. I stood the watch that morning while families across the country opened presents under trees. My wife at the time carried the weight at home. Handling bills, meals, and the loneliness, while I carried the rifle. When I finally walked through the door that morning, uniform damp from the cold, shoes stiff from the wet, she tried to make it feel like Christmas. But we both knew it wasn't the same. The Unknowns hadn't had Christmas either. That truth steadied me.

Thanksgiving was no different. While families sat down to turkey and laughter, Sentinels stood on the mat, stomachs empty, shoulders aching. In the quarters, meals weren't DFAC banquets. Most of the time, we brought our food with us. Cold leftovers stuffed into Tupperware or paper plates balanced on knees between shifts. But on occasion, the door would open and someone would walk in with generosity. Sometimes it was older badge holders, men who had walked the mat decades before, showing up with trays of food or home-cooked meals. Sometimes it was members of the Society of the Honor Guard, Tomb of the Unknown Soldier, who determined that no relief should feel forgotten on a holiday. They'd place the food down with a smile, exchange a few words, and leave us to it. The meal never lasted long. Guard changes and inspections didn't stop, but their kindness lingered. It reminded us that the brotherhood stretched beyond those currently serving.

Birthdays came and went the same way. I remember standing the watch on mine, boots clicking against the marble, watching the sun sink behind the amphitheater. Tourists didn't know, and they didn't need to. That was part of the sacrifice. Your personal milestones faded, swallowed by the larger duty of guarding the Unknowns.

The burden wasn't mine alone. Every Sentinel bore it. We all missed something. Holidays, anniversaries, first steps of children, phone calls from family. I remember brothers in arms who stood watch with the flu, running fevers under wool uniforms, unwilling to let the mat go unguarded. Others hid sprains or blisters so severe they bled through their socks, knowing that to complain was to fail the Unknowns. Sacrifice meant ignoring your own comfort, your own health, and sometimes even your own sanity.

The brotherhood carried us through. In the silence of the quarters, we shared unspoken glances of exhaustion that said, *I know. I'm with you.* A new guy struggling through uniform prep would get a quiet hand on his shoulder, or a badge holder would fix a crooked ribbon without a word. These were small sacrifices too—time, patience, encouragement—but together they built something bigger.

We gave up holidays, rest, and pieces of ourselves because the Unknowns had given everything. Compared to them, our sacrifices were nothing. But they were the way we lived out honor, day after day, one twenty-one-step walk at a time.

That was our duty. That was our honor.

The Tomb was not about us. It was never about the Sentinels. It was about the Unknowns, and the standard of honor their sacrifice demanded. Every step, every inspection, every sleepless night was our way of giving back in the smallest measure to men who had given all.

But the lessons of the Tomb did not stay locked within Arlington's chains. They followed me into the next chapters of my life, long after I left the mat behind. Honor and sacrifice shaped how I led, how I endured, and how I faced new challenges beyond the marble plaza.

When my orders came for the 101st Airborne Division, I carried the badge on my chest and the creed in my heart. The silence of Arlington would give way to the roar of training grounds and, eventually, the reality of combat. Yet the discipline, the reverence, and the standard remained the same. The watch had prepared me; now, life would test me in new ways.

Chapter 10 – Carrying It Forward

Even after leaving Arlington, the mentorship of Tomb Guards never stopped. The bond wasn't confined to the quarters or the mat. It extended into every stage of life. I had the privilege of learning from two men whose names carry immense weight in our community: Richard Azzaro, Badge #19, and Gavin McIlvenna, Badge #457.

Richard was among the earliest Sentinels to earn the badge, walking the mat in the 1960s when the Tomb was still shaping the traditions we now guard so carefully. He was also one of the four founders of the Society of the Honor Guard, Tomb of the Unknown Soldier, ensuring that the history, lessons, and spirit of the Tomb would be preserved for generations. Speaking with him, you realized quickly that for him, honor wasn't an abstract concept. It was a lived reality. His stories weren't grandiose or self-serving; they were reminders that the smallest details mattered because they were never about the guard. They were always about the Unknowns. I remember him saying once, "The Unknowns never asked for less, and neither should we." That single line has stayed with me ever since, a reminder that whether I was in uniform, in a classroom, or in a counseling office, the standard did not relax just because life had changed.

Gavin carried a different but equally powerful presence. Also, one of the Society's founders, his leadership ensured that the connection between generations of

Sentinels would never fade. Conversations with him were straightforward and direct, much like the corrections I had once received in the quarters. He emphasized that the badge was not just a personal achievement to be worn on your chest; it was a responsibility that extended outward. To educate, to mentor, to carry forward the legacy of the Unknowns. Gavin reminded me that our oath did not end when we left Arlington; it only transformed into new forms of service.

From both of them, I learned that being a Sentinel was never about the time you spent on the mat. It was about the life you carried after. Their mentorship made it clear that the badge was not just pinned once and forgotten. It was, and always would be, a covenant.

I still remember my final days in the quarters. Packing up my locker felt strange, almost hollow. For so long, every piece of cloth, every medal, every polished shoe had represented the constant pursuit of perfection. Now I was folding uniforms and taking down hangers, knowing that I would never again prepare them for the mat in the same way. Walking out of the quarters that last time, I felt the weight of silence differently. It wasn't the silence of discipline or the silence of a guard change. It was the silence of closing a chapter.

Touching the rail at the plaza one last time before I left marked a clear transition. Tourists would never know what it felt like to walk away after years of standing there, step after step, twenty-one forward, twenty-one back. To them, it was another ceremony they had witnessed. To me, it was the end of a life I had given everything to. It was also the beginning of the next test.

I will never forget my final walk at the Tomb. Fittingly, it was the last walk of the day, and it was also my 2,000th walk. No Sentinel had ever reached that number before. The cemetery had emptied, the crowds gone, and silence blanketed the plaza. As the sun sank low, the marble caught fire in the orange glow. Each step echoed across the stone with no other footsteps to accompany them. My rifle felt heavier that evening, as though it carried the weight of every walk I had taken before.

That number—2,000—wasn't about records or recognition. It was about endurance, about showing up day after day, year after year, and never lowering the standard. Each walk had been its own promise, a twenty-one-step vow to the Unknowns that they would not be forgotten. To have my final walk also mark that milestone felt less like an achievement and more like a closing circle, the end of a journey measured not in days but in steps.

When the walk was complete, I returned with roses in hand. Kneeling at the base of the Tomb and each crypt, I laid them down. My final tribute, my last act as an active Sentinel.

As I stood there, I thought about the journey itself. The seventeen men who had started with me and the few who remained, the blizzards and heat waves, the endless nights of polishing, memorizing, and testing myself against a standard that never bent. Every failure, every correction, every step on the mat had led to this moment.

When I laid the roses down, it was not for me or for anyone else. It was for the Unknowns alone. Their sacrifice, their silence, and their eternal vigil. It was my last duty as an active Sentinel, a final promise that they would never be forgotten.

It was a moment of mixed emotions. I felt honored to have served and done my time, and I was grateful for the chance to stand in that sacred duty. At the same time, there was a sense of relief that the burden was being passed on to the next group of soldiers who would take up the watch. For years, I had carried the weight of perfection, and now it would rest on their shoulders.

Alongside the relief and honor, nervousness set in as my next chapter approached. My orders were already in hand. The next step in my career was the 101st Airborne Division. I was leaving silence for chaos, marble for mountains, precision for uncertainty. As I stepped off the mat for the last time, I knew one chapter had closed, but the next would test me in ways I could not yet imagine.

When I arrived at the 101st Airborne Division, the shift was jarring. Arlington was defined by silence, precision, and discipline to the inch. A line unit was loud, chaotic, and unpredictable. Soldiers cursed openly, laughed, fought, and argued. Where the Tomb demanded that we stand in storms without moving, the 101st demanded that we move constantly. Through the mud, rain, long marches, and endless drills. The contrast was shocking, but the foundation I carried from the Tomb made me steady in the chaos.

At Arlington, precision meant survival. At the 101st, that same attention to detail kept men alive. The mat had taught me to endure discomfort, to focus under pressure, and to keep moving regardless of the conditions. In the field, that translated into never missing a check on my gear, never skipping over a detail in a plan, and never assuming that someone else had it covered. The Tomb had carved habits into me that became second nature.

Not everyone understood it at first. Some thought I was too rigid, too disciplined. I remember one soldier rolling his eyes when I re-checked my weapon after cleaning, muttering, "You already did that." Another laughed when I insisted on squaring away gear before a patrol. But over time, the same soldiers who mocked me came to appreciate it. A rifle inspected twice meant fewer malfunctions. A radio checked three times meant fewer communication failures. Slowly, respect replaced doubt. A standard carried from Arlington began to make sense in the dust and noise of Fort Campbell.

That habit—carrying the standard forward—became something I applied everywhere. Even in graduate school. There, I was surrounded by people who had never known the military. Most of my classmates had never worn a uniform, never stood in formation, never been tested in silence. They approached assignments casually, waiting until the last minute, cutting corners, or improvising when a structured approach would have served them better. For me, academics were easier. I treated them the way I had treated the mat: step by step, deliberate, disciplined. I didn't wait to start projects. I organized my time. I gave my best effort even when no one was looking.

That same discipline allowed me to maintain a high GPA, even though I was entering a field in which I had no prior experience: psychology. I learned that my so-called rigidity, which sometimes clashed with civilian culture, could actually be an asset. People appreciated me when I created structure, organized projects, and ensured things were done thoroughly. The balance came in learning to be flexible, too. To listen, to adapt, to adjust. It was the same lesson the Tomb had drilled into me in another way: precision matters, but so does humility.

Business was another challenge altogether. Founding my first company was like stepping onto the mat for the first time. The pressure was constant, the stakes were high, and failure was waiting at every corner. Just as I had once failed uniform inspections and knowledge recitations, I also failed in business. Deals fell through, clients disappeared, plans didn't work out. But the badge had already taught me that failure wasn't final. The only true failure was quitting. I refused to quit.

That mindset kept my first company alive past the fragile years when most small businesses collapse. Four years later, it still stood. Growth was slow, but it was steady. The lessons of the Tomb carried it forward: don't cut corners, don't lower the standard, never forget who you're working for. In the Tomb, it had been the Unknowns. In business, it was my clients, my employees, and the people who trusted me. The responsibility was different, but the principle was the same.

Even in the quiet hours, the Tomb shaped me. I developed a habit of reflection. Each morning, I took a moment to breathe and remind myself of the badge I had earned. I was no longer standing on the mat. Mentally, though, I still stepped into that role. I told myself, "Badge on." Simple. But it anchored me. It reminded me that perfection wasn't a one-time achievement. It was a standard that had to be pursued daily, no matter where I was.

That "badge on" mindset carried into fatherhood. Being a parent brought its own kind of inspections. Ones without checklists or uniforms, but no less demanding. Children don't measure you by your words but by your consistency. There were times I felt stretched too thin, times I worried I was failing them. But then I remembered the mat. I remembered the long nights when I wanted to quit, when every step felt like too much to bear. I hadn't quit then. I wouldn't quit now. Fatherhood, like Sentinel duty, required presence, patience, and the refusal to give up.

Carrying the badge also meant carrying honor. I knew what it was to stand for something greater than myself. In Afghanistan, that truth surrounded me. Brothers in arms, some who never made it home, reminded me that sacrifice wasn't history. It happened in real time. The Unknowns represented the fallen of past wars. Combat revealed that their story continued every time a soldier gave his life for another.

What the Tomb had taught me about honor and sacrifice became more than ceremonial words. They became lifelines in combat. When exhaustion clouded judgment, discipline cleared it. When fear tried to overwhelm me, ritual steadied me. When chaos surrounded me, I remembered the silence of the mat and found calm in the storm.

After the Army, resilience was needed in new forms. Education, business, and therapy all became crucibles in their own way. Long graduate school hours mirrored the endless nights of inspections and practice at Arlington. Writing a dissertation felt like memorizing knowledge pages. Painstaking, deliberate, requiring patience and persistence. Building two companies tested the same endurance as standing through the blizzard of 2009. Listening as a therapist demanded the humility I had learned during uniform inspections, when pride was stripped away and one had to face one's shortcomings honestly.

Circumstances changed. One principle remained: be present, be steady, never lower the standard.
For me, carrying it forward means ensuring the Unknowns are never forgotten. Not just at Arlington, but in every choice I make, every client I serve, every story I share. Their sacrifice reminds me that strength comes from discipline, resilience from struggle, and honor must guide all I do.

With Arlington having set my foundation, I faced a new beginning. The Tomb forged my discipline and sharpened my resilience, but now I would step into a new crucible: combat in Afghanistan, as a soldier with Easy (Alpha) Company, 2nd Battalion, 506th Infantry, 101st Airborne Division. The marble plaza would give way to the mountains and deserts of East Paktika, one of the most remote and volatile border regions of the war.

I remember reading the orders for Afghanistan and feeling the nervous anticipation churn inside me. Having left silence for chaos at the 101st, I now wondered if the discipline of the Tomb could hold up under fire. The mat had been a battlefield of patience and precision. East Paktika would be a battlefield of survival.

The silence of the mat would soon be replaced by the roar of gunfire and mortars, where the precision learned walking the plaza translated into handling weapons safely and efficiently. I didn't know then what lay ahead, only that the lessons of the Tomb had prepared me for it. Facing the relentless uncertainty of combat, I would learn just how deeply those lessons could withstand the chaos of war.

Conclusion

At the Tomb of the Unknown Soldier, I learned that perfection is not a destination but a daily standard. Honor and sacrifice shaped how I lived, led, and endured. Some duties do not end when you step off the mat; they carry forward into every chapter.

But my story did not end at Arlington. The badge was only the beginning. As I left the marble steps behind, I carried those lessons into Afghanistan. There, in Easy Company—the modern Band of Brothers—silence gave way to chaos, and sacrifice was no longer symbolic but immediate.

The Tomb had prepared me for what was to come. Afghanistan would test me, revealing how far a Sentinel's lessons could carry a soldier when the mat gave way to the battlefield.

And yet, beyond the battlefield, those lessons continue to guide me still. In every quiet morning before the world wakes, I hear echoes of the mat. Steady, deliberate, and unyielding. They remind me that purpose is not something left behind in uniform; it is something carried forward in how we live, serve, and remember.

For every Sentinel, the watch never truly ends. It lives on in the way we raise our families, lead our teams, and stand for those who can no longer stand for themselves. The mat may change, but the standard remains.

That is where the next story begins. With every step forged by honor, sacrifice, and an unending pursuit of excellence.

Copyright Page

The Mat Never Ends: Honor Beyond the Steps

Copyright © 2025 by SSG (R) Joseph L. Hull, LCSW

All rights reserved. No part of this book may be reproduced, stored in a retrieval system, or transmitted in any form or by any means, electronic, mechanical, photocopying, recording, or otherwise, without prior written permission of the copyright owner, except in the case of brief quotations embodied in critical articles, reviews, or educational use.

This is a work of nonfiction. All events and descriptions are based on the author's experiences. Some names and identifying details have been changed to protect privacy.

Published by Ironpath Publishing

Benton, Kentucky, United States

ISBN (Paperback): 979-8-218-82550-8

Cover design by SSG (R) Joseph L. Hull, LCSW

The Tomb Guard Identification Badge, The Old Guard, Arlington National Cemetery, and the Tomb of the Unknown Soldier are historical and institutional references; this book is not affiliated with, endorsed by, or officially connected with the U.S. Army, Arlington National Cemetery, or the Society of the Honor Guard, Tomb of the Unknown Soldier.

Dedication

To the Unknown Soldiers, your silence was my teacher. Every step I walked, every crease I pressed, every sleepless night in the quarters was for you. Though nameless, you remain unforgettable, and I will carry your memory until my last day.

To my fellow Sentinels, thank you for shaping me in ways words can never fully capture. You reminded me that perfection is not about pride, but responsibility, and that our standard lives long after we step off the mat.

To my grandfather and father, your quiet examples of service and sacrifice laid the foundation for everything I became. You taught me that honor is lived, not spoken.

To Gavin McIlvenna and Richard Azzaro, your mentorship has carried me far beyond Arlington's marble. You reminded me that the watch endures, even when we no longer wear the uniform.

To Lianè, thank you for standing by me through long nights of writing and doubt. Your encouragement reminded me that resilience is not carried alone.

And to my children, one day, you will read these words and understand why your father lived by a standard that never bent. Every sacrifice, every hour away, was so you would know the meaning of honor and the strength that comes from devotion.

www.ingramcontent.com/pod-product-compliance
Lightning Source LLC
LaVergne TN
LVHW012024060526
838201LV00061B/4448